KIDDING AROUND

TALES OF TRAVEL WITH CHILDREN

FOREWORD BY DERVLA MURPHY

HIGH LIFE HIGHLAND LIBRARIES	
38001900426051	
BERTRAMS	06/10/2019
910.83	£10.99
ANF	WITHDRAWN

Compiled and edited by
James Lowen and Hilary Bradt

Bradt

First published October 2019
Bradt Travel Guides Ltd
31a High Street, Chesham, Buckinghamshire, HP5 1BW, England
www.bradtguides.com
Print edition published in the USA by The Globe Pequot Press Inc,
PO Box 480, Guilford, Connecticut 06437-0480

Text copyright © 2019 Bradt Travel Guides (anthology) and © 2019 individual authors
(respective stories)
Introduction by Adrian Philips
Edited by James Lowen and Hilary Bradt
Proofread by Emma Gibbs
Cover design and concept by Cachete Jack
Typesetting by Ian Spick
Digital conversion by www.dataworks.co.in
Production managed by Sue Cooper and Jellyfish Print Solutions
Printed in the UK

All rights reserved. No part of this publication may be reproduced, stored in a retrieval
system, or transmitted in any form or by any means, electronic, mechanical, photocopying,
recording or otherwise without the prior consent of the publisher.

ISBN: 978 1 78477 105 8

Many thanks to the following: Eland Publishing Limited for permission to use an excerpt
from *Where the Indus is Young*, © Dervla Murphy (1977); and Adlard Coles Nautical, an
imprint of Bloomsbury Publishing Plc, for permission to use an excerpt from *Where the
Magic Happens: How a Young Family Changed their Lives and Sailed Around the World*,
© Caspar Craven (2018).

Photographs courtesy of authors, with the following exceptions: Astrid Vinje (page 75) by
Haner Photography; Amy-Jane Beer (page 96) by Lyndon Smith; Marie Kreft (page 207)
by Nichola Gotts Photography; and Lydia Unsworth (page 215) by Amy Macleod.

Contents

Foreword

Dervla Murphy

My mother believed in fresh air – really fresh, not contaminated by any form of indoor heating. Therefore throughout the first winter of my life (1931–2), most of my daylight hours were spent in the front garden when it was not raining and in the porch outside the hall when it was. Our co-tenants in that rambling old house on the edge of Lismore were appalled. Nowadays they would probably have reported my parents to the relevant authorities. Yet seventy years later, while travelling through Siberia in mid-winter, I observed many occupied cots and antique prams on the icicle-draped balconies of apartment blocks. The mothers explained that babies confined to overheated flats were usually sleep-deprived and fractious.

During my first journey beyond Europe, more than half a century ago, an odd fact puzzled me briefly. Citizens of the US, met on my travels, seemed pitifully prone to disease. How come? They were so rich, clean-smelling and equipped with novel hygiene aids. Then the dime dropped. They were *too* clean... Their immune systems had been compromised as they had grown up in an unnatural environment, chemically sprayed and scoured, where children were never allowed to eat bits of food retrieved off the floor.

Fast-forward to the 21st century. Us Oldies and many of our more sensible descendants are fretting about health and safety regulations imposed without intelligent debate. According to numerous recent reports, over-protected children are alarmingly stunted in their emotional (and increasingly their physical) development. Some primary schoolchildren of my acquaintance are not permitted to play outside if it's snowing. They might slip and hurt themselves. Or, the ultimate horror, be injured by classmates' snowballs. And yet the world is so out of joint that the same generation is often unprotected from internet pornography.

Alas and alas! The pernicious proliferation of motor transport really has made it unsafe, in built-up areas, for children to walk to school. Even where unnecessary, motorised school runs have become standard practice. Is walking as a means of travel now obsolete? In 1966–7, while trekking from Massawah (now Eritrea) to Addis Ababa (Ethiopia) through the then roadless Simien Mountains, I was accompanied by villagers whose five- or six-year-old children were capable of walking all day without complaint, covering fifteen miles or more. This observation was to prove immensely valuable during the years ahead. By 1973 I myself possessed one such creature on whom to experiment. That summer Rachel, aged four-and-a-half, walked eleven miles in a day. Until a few moments ago – historically speaking – most people had no choice but to walk to their destinations. And I myself, as an average adult, was able to enjoy walking 25 miles a day until my mid-seventies.

Over the next fourteen years, Rachel and I were to trek thousands of miles, usually with a pack animal, across three continents. Before our journeys, my particular style of mothering (ignoring health and safety diktats as well as school terms) met with little or no opposition from family and friends. However, my books each provoked a hail of critical bullets from shocked readers (mostly women). Several accused me of criminal irresponsibility. How dare I take a small child into isolated regions, beyond reach of modern communication and transport, for months on end? How could I be so cruel to that defenceless little girl?

All these kindly folk were missing a crucial point. In challenging circumstances, one's natural caution is sharpened while any reckless tendencies are blunted. Admittedly, caution is no bloody good if accident or illness strikes, so optimism must be part of the mix. While aware that the worst *could* happen, one remains irrationally confident that it *will not*.

To appeal to common sense signifies intellectual laziness, a reluctance or inability to muster a convincing argument. Or so I'm told. I always brandish that attribute when the argument is about risk and children. Previously the average parent was left to judge what was safe or unsafe for the average child. From the age of seven, during the summer holidays, I was free between sunrise and 6 p.m. to roam alone across fields, woods and mountainsides. But… until the age of twelve, I was strictly forbidden to swim alone in the River Blackwater, which was wide, deep and, in places, weed-infested. On weekdays I had to wait for my father to leave his office at 5 p.m. I was never tempted to disobey, despite already being a strong (if never stylish) swimmer. Even small children recognise common sense. Yet by the 1980s, thanks to over-protectionism, such normal swimming had been labelled absurdly as 'wild swimming'. It was assumed that paid coaches must give lessons in chlorine-polluted pools guarded by trained life-savers and furnished with vulgar chunks of plastic to enhance the young customers' enjoyment of tame swimming.

As the first cosseted generation became parents, then grandparents, the prevailing over-protectionism took its toll, and their offspring's natural development was increasingly inhibited. What passed for 'adventure travel' for this generation was really nothing more than a new type of package holiday, allowing truckloads of pioneering youngsters to 'discover' East Africa or the Himalayas.

In my family we did things differently – or tried to. In 2005, Rachel and I took her children to Cuba. We shared the blame for neglecting ten-year-old Rose, Clodagh (eight) and Zea (six). While foraging for ice cream not far from our lodgings, the Trio were allowed to find their adult-free ways around the streets of Havana, Santa Clara and Baracoa. We were reproached by a few twitchy gringos – but not by Cubans. Away from cities we were permitted in practice – though not in theory – to 'camp wild'. We found what, in my view, was an ideal campsite at the foot of the Sierra Maestra's highest ridge, five miles from the tiny village of Las Cuevas – a low headland overlooking a sandy cove.

Although this gratified the grown-ups, it transpired that the adaptability of modern children could fall short of that of their mother (and grandmother). Children of the noughties, it appeared, expected certain levels of comfort. 'There are lumpy stones under the grass,' Clodagh reported after an inspection. The Trio also demonstrated a lower risk threshold than their elders. 'It's not level,' Rose objected. 'We could roll over the edge while we're asleep.' Ignoring such concerns, the grown-ups unrolled five fleabags and announced that it was bedtime.

Come dawn, however, the others were no longer where their bags had been laid. Rachel had had a testing time overnight, coping with both paranoia about rolling off the cliff and absurd sensitivity to a few pebbles. And this was before the walk back. We followed an austerely beautiful corniche whose cliffs acted as storage heaters. Eight miles later, these threatened exhaustion as far as the Trio were concerned. 'Let's have a long rest,' begged Clodagh. 'Where?' demanded Rose.

'There's no shade.' 'I'm hot enough to *die!*' Zea announced. Children, it seems, are no longer built like they used to be.

All this said, very recently my attitude to certain everyday risks has been modified. Is this because age promotes prudence? Or are modern societies, in some respects, genuinely becoming more hazardous?

In 1986, Rachel spent her gap year travelling alone around India on a shoestring. (That shoestring has by now become a valued family heirloom; the Trio's enjoyment of travelling has never been diluted by affluence.) Having provided Rachel with letters of introduction to Tibetan friends in Mussoorie, I saw my ewe lamb off at London Heathrow and looked forward to our reunion the following year for a three-month trek in Africa, written up in my book *Cameroon with Egbert.* The internet manacle had not yet been invented, and we rarely communicated. Back then it seemed healthy for an experienced seventeen-year-old traveller to enjoy complete independence. But nowadays…?

Since 2014 Rachel has been based in India (in Dharamsala, scene of my second book, *Tibetan Foothold*). When the Trio visit her, she meets them in Delhi rather than allowing them to follow in her own solo footsteps across the subcontinent and through Himalayan fresh air. On one level, that relieves me: in today's world, Rachel's approach is safer than mine with her. However, on another level I am saddened by the changes – not least the negative potential of the internet – which have made such precaution seem sensible. Making such a mental adjustment is disagreeable. But one of the few advantages of being eighty-seven is that you can at least let your crankiness off the leash.

Read Dervla's story in this anthology on page 2.

Introduction

Adrian Phillips

Four years ago, my wife and I became parents. To twins. Double whammy. Yes, yes, I know the pleasures of parenthood can't be overstated, the joy unconfined and so on and so forth. But nor can the whammy-ness. Parenthood demands an overnight re-adjustment in your relationships towards almost everything, from sleep to work to socialising.

And of course to travel. In the early months and years, a simple trip to the supermarket requires military planning and saintly patience. Further down the track, the travel challenges change but are no less diminished, whether they involve persuading a ten-year-old to try the local cuisine or navigating the mood swings of an adolescent. They can chuck a bucket of cold water over any burning spirit of wanderlust.

But – because there are two sides to every dime, euro or dirham – those very challenges can also forge moments and memories around which you'll coalesce as a family for years to come. And that's what this book is all about. Some of the tales here are of family adventure, whether that features sleeping in the Jordanian desert, crossing the Gambia River in an overladen canoe, or getting profoundly lost on a Scottish mountain. Others relate voyages of parental learning that shine a light on what exploration means to a toddler or teenager. Then there are stories of disaster narrowly avoided: a lost child, a jet-ski accident, a jeep stuck deep in South African sand.

We ran a competition – promoted jointly with our friends at BritMums and Our Tribe Travels (about whom you can read more overleaf) – to find stories worthy of inclusion in this anthology. Some writers are seeing their work in print for the first time, while other tales that we have chosen to include were penned by professional writers. The contributors come from a range of backgrounds and tell of many different types of trip.

But they also share certain convictions: that parenthood doesn't mean abandoning those itinerant instincts; that, with the right attitude, even the most intrepid travel is possible with your family; and that the experiences of travel in childhood can shape personalities and inspire lives. Ultimately, whatever pitfalls they have encountered on the road, the contributors to this book know that travel is a portal to some of the most precious times that families can spend together.

Adrian Phillips is the Managing Director of Bradt Travel Guides, an award-winning travel writer and an exhausted parent. His confession of travelling ineptly with his children starts on page 36.

BritMums

Get out! That's great advice for every family – to travel and explore the world. At BritMums we're passionate about family travel. We love the way it educates, enlightens, invigorates and bonds us together. We're delighted to partner with Bradt Travel Guides, and to have helped gather family travel stories that are inspiring, amusing, quirky and thrilling.

BritMums is the UK's original influencer network, with 8,000 members. Our top-ranked website w britmums.com covers issues that affect modern parents and influencers, from personal stories to products to advice, spanning toddler to teenage years. On social media, follow @BritMums. Our co-founders write about family travel on their personal sites: Susanna Scott (w amodernmother.com; ➤ ◙ ℘ @amodernmother; ◪ @amodernmothertravels) and Jennifer Howze (w jenography.net; ➤ ◙ @JHowze; ◪ @Jenography; ℘ @jphowze).

Our Tribe Travels

Our Tribe Travels is a friendly global community of parents who favour a more adventurous style of travel. We share our tips and experiences to help others follow in our footsteps.

our tribe travels

Whether you want to explore India by rail, climb a mountain in Nepal, find a remote homestay in Australia's Northern Territory, drive across the USA or plan a round-the-world adventure, our online hub (w ourtribetravels.com; f ◎ ✈ @ourtribetravels) can connect you with someone who has done just that and can answer your family-travel queries.

Our members are based all over the world, from rural Ecuador to bustling Bangkok. It's this global footprint that also allows us to tap into local knowledge and reveal hidden gems. Want to explore the world with your kids? Come and join Our Tribe!

HIKES, HILLS AND WHEELS

Bedtime Stories
in Little Tibet

Dervla Murphy

One winter, Dervla Murphy and her six-year-old daughter Rachel, along with the pony Hallam, explored 'Little Tibet' high up in the Karakoram Mountains in the frozen heart of the Western Himalayas, on the Pakistan side of the disputed border with Kashmir. Dervla chose to travel in winter to avoid other tourists. For three months they travelled along the perilous Indus Gorge and into nearby valleys, beset by sub-zero temperatures, ferocious winds and whipping sands. Here are extracts from the resulting book, Where the Indus is Young.

* * *

From Chapter 2 – Dropped in the Indus Gorge

Our Christmas dinner consisted of chapattis and a watery dahl gruel, followed by watery tea. Seemingly they never rise to meat in Juglote, even for Id. But as this was our first meal in twelve hours it tasted remarkably good.

Then the proprietor led Rachel and me across a narrow yard to a room in which no progressive Irish farmer would keep pigs. The stone walls are smeared with dung and mud and for ventilation we have a tiny, high-up unglazed window and a 'chimney' hole in the roof. As I was reading Rachel her bedtime story (a ritual which unfailingly takes place in the most unlikely surroundings), we heard through the gloom weird, unhuman movements and utterances close beside us in this supposedly empty room. Rachel went rigid with fright and even I was momentarily unnerved. Then I resolutely swung my torch towards the sound – and discerned a speckled hen settled for the night on that pile of quilts and engaged in a vigorous flea-hunt.

From Chapter 3 – Alarms and Excursions

Two hours later we were on the edge of the gorge, and now my heart sank at the prospect of negotiating that unspeakable path. Akbar had gone far ahead with a friend. Holding Rachel's right hand (the drop was on our left), I moved down slowly and steadily, trying to keep my eyes off the river – which was not easy, since its noise and movement had a hypnotic effect. All went well until we came to a point some 250 feet above the water where the path simply ceases to exist. For perhaps two yards – only two brave, carefree steps! – one has to negotiate a cliff face on which a bird could hardly perch. This bulge overhangs the river so prominently that it is impossible not to look down, and my giddiness was increased by the sight of all those lumps of icy snow swirling and whirling below us. To circumvent it, one has to arch one's body outwards, while keeping one's head lowered to avoid the overhang, and there is no handhold of any kind.

As I crouched there, with one foot on the slippery polished rock, trying to work out how to get by without releasing Rachel's hand, a terrible, nightmarish paralysis suddenly overcame me. I felt that

I could neither go on, nor, because of Rachel, retreat up the path, which just behind us was only marginally less appalling. I realised that I had completely lost my nerve, for the first time ever, and it was an indescribably dreadful sensation – by far the most terrifying experience of a not unduly sheltered lifetime. The next stage (I was on the very verge of it) would have been pure panic and almost certain disaster. But then Rachel asked, altogether out of the blue as is her wont – 'Mummy, how are torpedoes made exactly?' And this question may well have saved our lives by momentarily taking my mind off the Indus.

I was afraid to turn my head, lest Rachel might be infected by the fear on my face. I simply gave my standard reply to such technological questions – 'I've absolutely no idea, darling' – and the sound of my own voice uttering those familiar words at once steadied me. As Akbar stared at us from the landing-stage I shouted, 'Please take Rachel!' and he raced up the cliff. I passed Rachel to Akbar across that horrific stretch of non-path and the moment she was safe regained my nerve. But I shall never forget those paralysed moments.

From Chapter 11 – Kiris to Skardu
Skardu – 10 March

This morning saw an historic event of enormous interest: the removal by the Misses Murphy of their clothes, after almost three months. Rachel was disappointed – 'Our bodies don't look dirty! It's all on our vests!' Apparently one does not get progressively dirtier in a very cold climate. That protective coating of oil which establishes itself on the skin seems to repulse dirt. There was of course nothing to be done with our underclothes but drop them on the midden outside, from where they will soon be retrieved by some fuel-hunter.

From Chapter 12 – Spring comes to the Shigar Valley

Shigar – 19 March

Among the glories of this Rest House is a roll of pale pink loo-paper, left here last summer by one of the tourists (an American girl and a Frenchman) entered in the Register for 1974. Rachel asked excitedly, 'How did this get here?', and when I explained she curled her lip. 'They must've been cissies to put *loo paper* in their luggage!'

'It doesn't follow,' I said mildly. 'Not everyone has been brought up the hard way, on snowballs and stones.'

Life in Baltistan certainly teaches one to adapt a few possessions to many uses: I can think of no better antidote to the West's gadget demented subculture. Our sack, for instance, is officially a sack – if you follow me – but in its off-duty hours it becomes, according to prevailing conditions, a window-curtain, a tablecloth, a mattress, a pillow, a horse blanket or a floor-covering to protect new Rest House carpets from my culinary activities. Similarly, the lid of the old Complan tin used as a tea-caddy also serves as a mirror (the inside) and a candle holder (the outside), while our nailbrush serves as clothes-brush, saucepan-cleaner, boot-brush and potato scrubber, and our *dechi* as wash-up basin and, *in extremis*, as chamberpot. Possibly the time is nearer than we think for the Western world to learn how expendable are most of its newfangled gadgets.

Skardu – 21 March

For us Now Ruz ended on a sordid note, Rachel was abed and I had just begun this entry when a pathetic small voice said, 'What's biting me doesn't feel like fleas'. I took up my candle to examine the victim and the bites did not look like fleas, either. So I lit another candle, the better to hunt and found Rachel's clothes literally crawling with tiny grey body-lice. This was an extremely serious situation. I threw away all those filthy garments we removed before going to Shigar, so at present we have only the clothes we stand up (and lie down) in. Having made sure that the victim's skin was lice free, I thrust her, naked and shivering, into my flea-bag. Body-lice are well named; there was not one louse on her pants, tights and stockings, despite the swarming mass of grey horrors on her upper garments. I dropped the infested clothes in a far corner of the field; first thing tomorrow they must be boiled. I find I react quite differently to fleas and lice. There is something so irresistibly comical about fleas that one can feel no real animosity towards them; a flea hunt is a form of sport, demanding considerable skill, and one has to admire the creatures' cheeky agility. But those slow grey crawlers this evening really revolted me.

Reprinted from *Where the Indus is Young* by Dervla Murphy, by kind permission of Eland Publishing Limited, 61 Exmouth Market, London EC1R 4QL. © Dervla Murphy 1977

Dervla Murphy was born in 1931 in Ireland. In 1963 she cycled to India where she worked with Tibetan refugee children. Her first book, *Full Tilt: Ireland to India with a Bicycle*, was published in 1965. Over twenty titles have followed and she has won worldwide praise for her writing. Now in her eighties and still living in County Wexford, Dervla remains passionate about travel, politics, conservation, bicycling and beer.

David's First Glimpse
of Eternal Snows

Jane Wilson-Howarth

The consultant – with his comet's tail of junior doctors, medical students and nurses – came into David's little hospital side-ward and sat Simon and me down. Consultants don't usually take time to sit and talk. He plunged straight in. 'The tests... You know that we have identified quite a list of problems. Your baby's intellectual development is not going to be normal... It is important that he has surgery on his heart very soon. We need to do more tests to see exactly what else is wrong.'

I was reeling, speechless. Despite being a doctor, I couldn't challenge the experts who were in charge of my month-old son's life. I did manage to ask: 'Will David walk... or even talk? I'm not sure about the surgery. Not sure it will really help him.'

We weren't convinced these clever British doctors had David's quality of life in mind and, after much soul-searching, discharged him from hospital and fled back to Nepal where Simon, his father, was working.

Away from hypodermics and nasogastric feeds, David rallied and put on weight. Then, when he was just over three months old (and his brother Alexander was three years), the Desain festival came around, prompting Simon to take some time out. We flew to Pokhara and set off on a teahouse trek. Even our Nepali friends questioned the wisdom of such a trip with the children but we needed some healing mountain air after the emotional turmoil of David's first weeks.

Most treks start steep and this was no exception. Alexander and Simon were soon skipping up huge, uneven stone steps. Porter Chhetra Bahaadur followed carrying David in a conical bamboo basket, lying comfortably on his supply of Pampers and sheltered from the sun by a cloth supported by hoops of bamboo. Kesab (carrying our luggage) and I (carrying only camera and water bottle) laboured at the back. The physiotherapist's advice after my caesarean section was to build up activities with the aim of being able to hoover the stairs after three months. She probably would have disapproved.

The first village of Dhampas was a tough 1,500-metre slog above our starting point. Only when we came out on to this first grassy ridge could I properly take in the scenery. 'So was that climb more strenuous than hoovering the stairs?' Simon teased.

I didn't have the energy to respond with any more than a hands-on-hips glare. He went on, 'Nice view, eh?' Then, 'No: look up!' Emerging above the clouds was the towering amphitheatre of the Annapurna horseshoe and, nestling inside, the stately pyramidal peak of Machhapuchharé, the fishtail.

'Wow! What's my favourite mountain doing up there?' I said. 'It seems so close. Look how the snow glistens and the ice sparkles. And how blue the sky is!'

Villagers came to peek under David's sunshade-cloth. '*Such* white skin!' Proud-father-like Chhetra fielded questions about David who, responding to his new celebrity status, burbled happily. How Nepalis love comparing babies! Even the checkpost policemen were delighted to meet the kids and chat. Trekkers consistently ignored the boys, though, and while Alexander socialised happily with Nepalis, he soon concluded that European adults were not worth even a hello.

Our route took us up along the ridge, then down into a steep, densely forested valley echoing with birdsong. Alexander and Simon would often branch off on a game of chase, then I'd hear the sound of a small boy making motorbike noises and Alexander would come running past. I was pacing myself better by now, but only when I stopped (to feed David or catch my breath) did the world really come back into focus. Even so, I could set my own rhythm, resting when I wanted. I was loving this trek; how awe-inspiring it was to be in among these mountains and the majestic forest.

David's conical basket looked precarious when 'parked', so while I prepared his food I propped him in a triangle made by resting my right ankle on my left knee, where I could bounce him. He would coo and chat while I ground up his heart medicines or mixed baby rice. He was content and peaceful now that he was no longer a clinical object in a high-tech teaching hospital but surrounded by love and admiration. It was wonderful watching him tune in to interesting noises and laugh at bellowing buffaloes or cranky cockerels.

We climbed high so that the river, now way below us, sounded like a distant raging beast. There were tree ferns, huge hemlocks festooned with orchids, staghorn ferns and mosses, patches of intoxicatingly perfumed daphne twittering with tiny colourful birds, purple primroses and delicate violets poking out of rocky crevices. We would reach the top of a ridge only to descend, then up and up again.

As I panted into the hamlet of Jhinu, Chhetra asked: 'You like hot bath, *memsahib*?' I wasn't keen to make any detours, but a hot spring was irresistible. Chhetra led me through thick forest where boiling sulphurous water had been cleverly diverted to mix with the right amount of river water, creating a pool at perfect bath temperature. David chuckled as he kicked his seldom-used legs. Only after we'd been soaking for a while did I notice that we were being watched by a troop of langurs with long, furry bell-pull tails browsing in trees that overhung the river. When I smiled at the lookout, he looked away and examined his fingernails.

Sometimes I'd walk right behind Chhetra, listening to David babbling softly. Sometimes I'd lag behind and on catching up ask, 'How is he?'

'My Dabid is fast-asleeping.' Then again I'd follow for a while and the next time I caught them up, I'd hear David burbling contentedly while Chhetra sang and chatted amiably back, 'Be happy, Dabid!'

I staggered into the Annapurna View Lodge and immediately saw Alexander running in the garden. I slumped on to a bench hoping I'd never need to get up again. Simon (with David in his arms and Alexander at his heels) planted a kiss on my steaming forehead and thrust a hot lemon drink into my hand. 'You made it!' he said.

Alexander chipped in. 'Look, I've got this shiny steering wheel.' And he put his imaginary car into gear and drove off using a metal plate to steer. By now, he knew how to ask politely in Nepali for an empty plate wherever we stopped. 'What shall we eat? I'll skip the Vegetable Craps. Mixed Tonic Soup sounds just what I need.'

I looked out at the spectacular mountain scenery. Annapurna South looked hardly a stone's throw away. The Patal Ganga Glacier slid, cracked and jerked painfully downwards like an old arthritic beast. An avalanche poured off the mountain. 'How close Machhapuchharé looks now!' I said. 'And how it's dwarfed by the Annapurnas.' The superb angular pinnacle peeked out shyly from the clouds; the jet stream blew snowy spindrift from knife-edge ridges.

From Ulleri we climbed to 3,000 metres but then the path took us right down to the Kali Gandaki. Having reached the river, we climbed again, only to descend further on. Alexander motored on, giving us anxious moments when he practised three-point turns close to precipitous edges. David babbled, cooed and chuckled, or slept. Chhetra never hesitated as he plodded surefootedly onwards.

As we walked up through Ghasa's steep main street, a drunk staggered up and lunged at Alexander, intending to tweak his cheek. But, well used to what he considered a wholly bad Nepali habit, Alexander skilfully dodged, and then wandered off and joined another group of kids.

I noticed a child with cerebral palsy was watching us. He was about ten years old and had been left out to bask in the sun while his cousins and neighbours played around him. He was part of the community, well cared for, involved. In the West disabled folks tend to be out of sight. He wasn't hidden away, so every day he showed those without a handicap what life is like for the disabled.

An avenue of long, thin, vertical prayer flags led us to a courtyard painted with scary protector deities. 'Ooh, can I bang the gongs?' Alexander enthused. The smiling *lama* who ushered us into the scented gloom showed Alexander how to make the most noise, encouraging him to hit every drum and then spin a gaudy three-metre-high prayer wheel that rang a bell every time it turned.

There were now pine trees growing wherever the slope would allow. We were getting high again and as the gorge cut between two 8,000-metre peaks the sun seldom reached us. We basked like lizards wherever we could find a patch of sun, although when I breastfed David I'd sit with my back to the rays so that it warmed me without dazzling him.

The wind got up as the sheer, stark valley began to open out. Locals said that this was normal in the upper Kali Gandaki valley and made landing light aircraft hazardous. There was one nose-down in the river at the end of the runway at Jomsom. Alexander was disappointed when the next plane didn't crash.

Beyond Jomsom was a wasteland of cobbles in a wide flood plain. We'd crossed the Himalayan watershed and reached the desert of the Tibetan Plateau. After nearly a fortnight of walking we were rewarded by being sandblasted with a biting, dust-laden wind. Alexander didn't care though, and David was cosily tucked up in his big bamboo basket under a large bath towel. He kept up long burbling conversations with himself. If he seemed unsettled, Chhetra would say, 'Be happy, Dabid!' and sing him a song.

We approached Kag Beni, the fortress town controlling trade north to south, and ducked through a low gateway topped by a huge breast-shaped *stupa*. We'd plunged into a labyrinth of alleys and tunnels between cram-packed houses. It felt and smelt medieval.

A group of women were sitting in the sun, spinning. They spotted Alexander and called us over, then giggled with delight when they noticed David. 'Take him out! Let us see him! We must hold him!' Then, 'What beauty he has, *didi*! *Ah-mai*, his harelip is invisible!'

Next day was a tough climb from 2,800 metres up a side valley to Muktinath at 3,800 metres; we escaped the wind but the air was so thin, my lungs felt no bigger than a dog's scrotum. Below, the river sparkled like cut glass. The sun spotlit lines of deep-green pine trees on the interlocking spurs that had forced the river into meanders. The valley and mountains above were spectacularly folded, and coloured by metal ores; subtle red, purple, orange, green, bluish and heron-grey strata were stacked like playing cards. The landscape of scree and crags had a stark grandeur that moved me.

Finally, we reached Muktinath, which nestled among poplars. We'd followed the route used by pilgrims and ascetics from India since 300BC. Here, each chilly dawn, fasting devotees bathe in ice-cold water that pours from 108 carved-stone cow-head spouts and pray at the holy, natural-gas flame.

Simon told Alexander a bedtime story about Goldilocks and the three yetis and he was soon sound asleep. But that cold, cold night I lay awake listening to my older son's erratic breathing. I knew this was due to the altitude but that didn't stop me worrying. At least delicate David was fine; holes in his heart made him make an excess of red blood cells which protected him. I hardly slept. Deciding we'd go no higher was sensible.

Next morning, we started down, nibbling on a new supply of tangy dried apricots. I was fitter now and the way seemed easier. On the nineteenth day, we reached the road and caught a dilapidated 'Super Sonic' night-express bus to Kathmandu.

Simon hadn't needed to carry Alexander much. He had walked half the hundred miles of the trek – and he'd enjoyed it. We all had. Even David, with his delicate stomach, light-sensitive eyes and weak heart, had been animated by the trip. He was no longer the nervous twitchy baby of the awful hospital weeks when they took blood from him daily. In England people saw he was 'not right' and looked away. In Nepal they saw his differentness as being touched by the gods, and admired his easy, chuckly personality and blonde curls. Not only that, but he never did need the heart surgery the consultant thought so urgent. He healed the holes himself.

We celebrated our return to Kathmandu by buying the book *Tintin in Tibet*. Alexander was pleased, for it contained all the elements of our adventure: rocky paths, snowy mountains, lamas, gongs, drunks, yaks and a plane crash, as well as a kindly yeti. Alexander wanted to know when we'd be going trekking again. 'Soon,' we replied. And we did. During nearly six years in Nepal we completed a dozen family treks, some of which were a month long.

This excerpt is adapted from *A Glimpse of Eternal Snows*, published by Bradt Travel Guides in 2012. **Dr Jane Wilson-Howarth** also co-authored Bradt's e-book *Your Child Abroad: a Travel Health Guide*. Jane is a British medical doctor who has served as a GP in Cambridge but once again is living and working in Nepal. She has written nine books, including two wildlife adventures for children set in Nepal. Her author website and blog is at **w** www.wilson-howarth.com.

Taking the Teen for a Walk

Jude Marwa

The three of us standing at the front door have been ready to leave for some time. Our backpacks are on, and our boots are laced. We're just waiting for Maia.

Our teenage daughter's refusal to leave her room has put us an hour behind schedule. Eight-year-old Silas is particularly miffed. He can't understand why our hike along the South Downs Way has to involve all four of us. 'I knew she'd ruin it. This was meant to be our thing, Mum.'

My husband Emil nods. 'It'll be dark by the time we reach Pyecombe if we wait much longer.'

The prospect of the four of us arguing our way over the downs for three days isn't my idea of fun either. An international move, new schools and jobs have taken their toll, meaning that we *need* this break.

'It will be brilliant once we get going,' I smile.

The bedroom door swings open and Maia stomps her way down the stairs. She throws on her backpack and glares at me, her face blotchy and wet with tears.

'If anyone sees me on this hike I just want you to know my life will be hell forever and it'll all be your fault. And I haven't even got any socks on because you didn't care enough to buy me the right socks for this stupid, humiliating walk.'

Idyllic! Perfect! Such were my thoughts when planning this trip. We'll be able to walk to the South Downs Way from our own front door in Brighton. But as we trudge the first five miles alongside the noisy A27, it feels far from perfect, the opposite of idyllic.

The concrete underfoot is unforgiving and by the time we turn off on to our first stretch of grass, the soles of our feet are already tender and blistered. The relief of swapping concrete for mud is slightly clouded by a signpost that says 'Longhill.' I look up. It is well named. They've just missed out the words 'flipping steep'.

We climb up the narrow, near-vertical path and pause under a tree for a snack. Our first view across the rolling fields of Sussex is breathtaking. The warmth of the spring sun teases us into thinking that everything is going to be calm and bright from here on in.

Silas chatters away about the route ahead as he munches on a small Snickers bar. Maia sits apart, her back to us, hoodie drawn tightly around her head.

Suddenly she gets up and starts off again on her own.

'Wait, let's check the guidebook and see which way the route goes,' Emil calls out. Maia shrugs. 'Or we could just follow the signs that say South Downs Way,' she remarks with harsh scorn.

Our route changes to rugged chalky paths, with open grassland stretching out beyond. The bursts of yellow flowers adorning the gorse bushes bring dashes of warmth and hope.

As we pass the high point of Black Cap, a family of rabbits hops by. I'm reminded of the times when Maia was little and I'd drive us both up to the fields at the top of our road. We'd sit in pyjamas, eating sandwiches – just the two of us – waiting for the rabbits to come out for their evening feed. I notice Maia stopping to look at the rabbits as well. The tightness of her hood lends her cheeks a toddler's roundness.

Her feline eyes and faintly freckled nose haven't changed much since she was tiny.

After a long meander along the uneven ridge path, we stop for lunch close enough to a pine forest to discern its distinctive scent. Dramatic valleys plunge away to our left. Surrounded by glorious scenery, an irresistible sense of freedom surges in.

We've walked over halfway, but the sun is already fading and clouds are rolling our way. Ahead I can see Ditchling Beacon with its collection of day trippers. We often drive up here from Brighton, just to sit and let the wind knock us about.

'Are you kidding? We're only *here*? What was the point in all that walking? We could have just driven here!' Maia is unamused.

It starts to rain, and the wind really picks up. Maia is even less amused. 'Great. Just so you know, everyone here is thinking "Look at those idiots with their bags and boots, like they think they're hiking in the Himalayas." We could literally get the bus home right now. Why can't we just be a *normal* family and do *normal* things?'

God, it's tempting to hitch a ride back to Brighton. But I grit my teeth and smile. 'Come on, kids. We're about four miles from where we'll be staying tonight. We can do this.'

Up here you feel like you are on top of the world. On a calm day you can imagine rolling down the hill and being caught by a soft blanket of grass at the bottom. Today, though, it feels more like we are about to be torn from the hillside and violently hurled into the valley.

Silas crouches near the ground and starts to cry. Maia turns; I think she is about to shout at him for being a baby. Instead she holds his hand and pulls his arms out like wings. 'Fall back and the wind will catch you. It's OK, I've got you. Look, it's holding me, Silas! Look! AAAAGGGHHHH, it's actually holding me! I'm putting all my weight against it. I'm literally lying down in the wind. Try it, go on, it's so cool!'

Emil and I stand together watching our children giving themselves to the wind, squealing as it threatens to let them fall. I pocket the moment.

A few miles through the storm and we reach two windmills cutely named Jack and Jill, which stand at the edge of the hamlet of Pyecombe. In the dip of the land, the wind dies down. We have done day one. We've survived a storm. We've survived each other and we've earnt a hearty meal and a restful night in our B&B.

'What's the name of the B&B?'

Oh Jesus, I have no idea. I booked it weeks ago and felt so proud of myself for having organised things so far in advance that I hadn't given it another thought since. I extract my phone to Google it and, as I look at the screen, it dies.

'Uh-oh. Typical. Someone must have unplugged my phone this morning. Can I use yours, Emil?'

'Mine died ages ago.'

'Oh great. Well, this is perfect isn't it?' Maia says. 'Well done, Mum, for banning me from even bringing mine.'

Now it's Silas's turn to lose heart. 'Mum, please can we just stay somewhere now. I'm exhausted.'

'Shh! Let me think. I'm trying to remember if it actually was in Pyecombe? Maybe it was Poynings...'

'Oh my God. We're not even in the right village. Where the heck is Poynings? I just want to go home. My legs hurt.'

Now it's Emil's turn to glare at me. 'You really have no idea where we're staying?'

'Well, in my defence...'

'No, Jude! There is no "defence" for leaving the house without any idea of the name of the B&B, or even what sodding village it's in.'

'We can just book another one here, and I'll have to pay again.'

I rummage around in my bag and pockets, but there's just no sign of what I need. I'm losing face at breakneck speed.

'Emil, did you take my purse out of this bag?' He rolls his eyes: 'No!'

'Well *someone* did, because it's not here.'

The children fall apart in a blur of exhausted tears and furious accusations. I look around the minute settlement. I could actually knock on every door until I find the bloody B&B.

I walk up a garden path.

'Hello, I'm sorry to bother you. I've booked us into a B&B tonight, but I can't remember the name of it. Did I book us in here?'

'No.'

'Do you know of any other B&B's in the village?'

'There are lots down that hill.' The lady shuts the door.

'We've got to walk to Poynings,' Maia says assertively. 'I know because you tried to bribe me by saying we could have lava cake and ice cream at the Royal Oak. And the Royal Oak is in Poynings. Not Pyecombe.'

We leave Pyecombe behind and cross the A23. Cars zoom underneath us, scores of drivers who are almost home. At the end of a bridleway is the entrance to the next leg of the walk. Another steep climb. We walk on in silence. Dusk starts to fall. At the top of the next ridge, I look back at Brighton.

'Just look at that sunset!'

I am heartened by the responses.

'Brighton looks really pretty like that. I love this time of day. It reminds me of Christmas.'

'I guess we'd have missed this if you'd remembered to bring your purse, charge your phone or had any idea of where the hell we were staying, Mum.'

A mile or two along the open, grassy path, the spectacular view of Devils Dyke starts to come into view. Suddenly the instructions in the guidebook become confusing.

'I'm telling you, this is the path. Look at the lights down there. That's Poynings,' urges Maia.

'But that's not what the book says.'

'It is, it so is. It's just that it's pitch-black now and you can't see anything.'

We turn off down the path that Maia has found. 'Mum, I'm scared. It's so dark. I'm going to trip and die.' I am in total agreement with Silas. 'Don't worry. I have a torch in my pack.' I seize my chance to recoup some respect. 'Aha, and here it is. Oh. Which one of you took the damn batteries out?'

Wet, muddy and a little bit scratched, each of us picks ourselves up at the bottom of the path. And as we do I am grateful for the next sight. 'That's the village! We're here! We just climb over that stile and that's it, we've done it!'

Maia is first over the stile – and first to report back. 'That light. It's not the light from the village. It is the reflection of the moon on an effing lake.' It is the first time we have ever heard her swear.

We walk on but any peace that could have been found in the stillness of the night is demolished by the awful sounds of broken children limping and crawling to the end of a 17-mile hike.

Then we turn a corner and this time we really are there.

Friendly chatter rises up to meet us as we fall into the Royal Oak. I lean on the bar where words spill incoherently from my mouth.

'I've booked something somewhere. A table and a bed. We are late. I'm dehydrated.'

'Is there a B&B near here, please?' Maia takes over.

'There is, yes. Four hundred metres southwest of here.'

'Thank you.' And we leave the pub.

'Which way is southwest?' Maia asks.

'I have absolutely no idea,' I reply. Maia looks at me 'Who even says that? We're not Scouts.'

Emil calls out to us from across the road. 'I've found it!' We race towards his voice and find him with a friendly-looking lady.

'I was so worried about you all! You were supposed to be here hours ago. Once it got dark, I tried to call but your phone had no connection. I didn't know quite what to do. Anyway you're here now, and very tired, I expect.' We follow her into her house through the stable door. 'Mum, this place is so cute! I love it,' Maia coos.

Later, back in the Royal Oak, warmed by the fire and relieved to learn we can pay for dinner via bank transfer, we recover. Lava cake and ice cream arrive at the table. Maia smiles and picks up our copy of the *Guide to the South Downs Way*.

'So, where are we headed tomorrow?'

Jude Marwa is a teacher who lives and works in Singapore with her husband and two children. She loves to write and is proud to have a second story published by Bradt Travel Guides. She considers life in southeast Asia to be wonderful, but still reckons that you can't beat standing on top of a British hill on a windy day.

Harriet's First Trek

Matthew Ellis

Harriet was four months old, we were living and working in Nepal, it was September and we were marking the beginning of the trekking season with our first family trek. Sensible of my new role as a first-time father, we were going with a local trekking company that was taking a small group of like-minded expat residents on a mid-altitude, week-long trek a few hours' drive to the east of Kathmandu. What could possibly go wrong?

I watched a man casting a fishing net into the river as we waited for oncoming traffic at a one-way stretch of the 'highway' that leads up to the Friendship Bridge and the crossing point from Nepal into Tibet. With the tingling feeling that comes with departures on journeys I inwardly celebrated our escape from the Kathmandu Valley and looked forward to the adventure ahead. Our destination was to be the sacred peak of Kalinchowk (named for the goddess Kali worshipped at the summit shrine). We would reach this halfway round a circular route up a long forested ridge from the valley of the Sun Kosi – which was where I had watched the old man fishing.

At the roadhead, by a huddle of mud-walled houses with corrugated-iron roofs, 'would-be' porters swarmed around the battered minibus as the baggage was passed down from the vehicle roof and sorted into loads. There, as promised, was a basket for the baby, complete with a headstrap which was soon strung around the brow of Ram Bahadur, the trusted Kathmandu team member deputed to carry Harriet. Once settled on a little padded mattress tucked in by a cotton blanket and swung up effortlessly to hang from Ram's head, she looked 'as snug as a bug in a rug'. As we set off up the path, I positioned myself strategically behind Ram, seeking reassurance that Harriet was in safe hands (or, rather, on a safe head!). I needn't have worried as Ram climbed steadily, footsure up the typically steep ascent over rough ground with stretches of the red mud I always associated with the memorable Nepali warning epithet *'raato mato, chiplo baato'* ('red earth, slippy path'). So I could relax and enjoy the scenery. We were climbing a *lekh* (ridge) up into thick forest above the river that was glinting in the late-afternoon light below.

The tents had already been pitched when we entered the clearing for our first night's sleep. We had been assigned a comfortable three-person dome tent and went to collect our gear from the baggage pile. There was our barrel bag containing clothing and wash bags... but where was the baby's bag with all the nappies? We were not the only members of the party to be missing stuff. It didn't take long for suspicion to focus on the rather disreputable local 'porters' offering their services during the confused unloading process. Our *sirdar* (senior porter) went back down to negotiate with the locals and returned having managed to locate some of the missing luggage. Nevertheless, despite his best efforts, it appeared that the baby's nappy bag had proved just too desirable to be found. No need to panic: we still had the reusable nappy she was wearing and, with a little improvisation, had enough soft material to replace the lining as long as we made time for some unplanned washing en route. The trip was getting more authentic by the day!

The following morning dawned soggily. The monsoon rains that were due to have finished clearly had not read the script. I hadn't bargained for trekking through the rain. Appearing at the tent door with cups of tea and a sheet of plastic, Ram reassured us that he would be able to keep the baby dry regardless of the weather. Sure enough, as we struck camp and I again fell in behind him and Harriet, I saw she was cosily sheltered under a plastic sheet. This was cleverly suspended from Ram's headstrap so that it draped around the sides of the basket – allowing the rain to run off harmlessly wide of the basket.

For Harriet's parents at least, it was a long damp day as we climbed the ridge cloaked in thick cloud with the steady monsoon rain dripping off the trees around us. By late afternoon the cloud had lifted sufficiently for glimpses of Gauri Shankar, a 7,000-metre-high peak towering just east of us. Our campsite that night was dank and dark as we arrived, but soon brightened up as our resourceful crew got a fire going, food on and distributed much-needed Khukri rum rations. By bedtime the stars were shining brilliantly down on our little clearing where the flickering light of the fire created a shadow play on the tent walls. It was time to gear up for a better day, including the crux of the hike – panoramic views from the mountaintop temple of Kali. But as I retired to my sleeping bag I lay listening to a series of coughs from Harriet. These were both new and rather alarming.

I had come to Nepal with five years specialist training in paediatrics. I was well aware that respiratory symptoms are by far and away the commonest medical complaint during early childhood. During long nights in the casualty department and walking the wards, I had heard literally thousands of coughs. The hawking associated with bronchiolitis is characteristically dry, wheezy and rasping. I had worryingly little doubt that this was Harriet's direction of travel.

After a night punctuated by the baby's coughing fits, the following day dawned bright and set fair. A couple of middle-class Nepali men swung by the camp carrying a chicken by the legs, greeting us in a friendly manner. As our party tucked into breakfast, a medical consultation was held in our dome tent as Harriet's mother (a GP) and I took stock of the situation. On the plus side, Harriet had managed her morning feed and wasn't in respiratory distress, the weather was fine and we were within striking distance of the summit. On the minus side her cough had definitely worsened overnight, we were half-a-day's walk plus the same drive away from any medical facility where oxygen would be available – and the plan was for the trek to take a further three days.

In consultation with our *sirdar*, a shorter way back down to the road was agreed. Yes, of course Ram Bahadur could peel off with us. Decision made – we could take in the summit and, in just three more hours, descend to the road where we would just have to hitch a ride back to the city. Time was now of the essence so we got ourselves rapidly organised, said our farewells and set off with the ever-reliable Ram leading the way.

In glorious morning light we were soon on the summit, which was bedecked with Shiva tridents reflecting Mother Kali's status as the consort of Lord Shiva. Kali is a blood-drinking deity so we waited respectfully as the chicken-toting Nepalis encountered earlier completed their blood sacrifice – that particular fowl wouldn't be crossing any more roads. The fleeting thought crossed my mind that these guys looked like townies in a hurry; perhaps they had transport down on the road?

As we congregated at the seasonal teahouse below the summit, I used my best Nepali to explain our predicament and enquire as to the possibility of a lift. Yes, came the response: the men had a Tata Land Cruiser down on the road below and would be pleased to give us a lift with the baby. They would, however, have no room for Ram. I explained the situation and Ram was immediately gracious in his reassurance. He agreed that getting the baby back home was the priority. If necessary, he could ride back on the roof of a weekend bus.

Late that evening our new friends dropped us outside our Kathmandu flat, whereupon I sat up nursing a coughing and increasingly distressed baby for much of the night. Fortunately, Harriet's bronchiolitis improved over the next few days without the need for oxygen. Nevertheless, it was a close-run thing the next night when she developed respiratory distress, tugging in her soft breastbone with every hard-fought breath.

Travelling with a young child – particularly an adventurous journey along the lines of a trek – is a marvellous shared experience, but not without its complications. As we learned on Kalinchowk, you have to plan sensibly and stand ready to cut your losses if things don't turn out as expected.

Harriet became ever more integrated into Nepal. Her first word some months later was *dudh* (milk) and the following trekking season saw me carry her halfway up Everest (the easier half!). While lugging her on my back as I made the stiff climb from Lukla towards Namche Bazar I became aware of looks of disapproval from some older trekkers that culminated in a frank warning. If they were struggling upwards while suffering the ill-effects of mild altitude sickness, what was I doing there with a *baby*? What my critics did not know was that – unlike them – Harriet and I had trekked in from Paphlu, several days down the valley, and were properly acclimatised.

Along our approach, we enjoyed a memorable audience with Trulshik Rimpoche at Thupten Choling Monastery, following his relocation from the famous Rombuk Monastery on Everest's north side. Rimpoche asked for Harriet to be placed on his knee. As he was enjoying her smiling attention, a muffled explosion indicated that nature had taken its course. The rather rancid odour of yak-butter tea was now overlain with something pungently sweeter. Thankfully, on this occasion, Harriet's nappy was firmly in place. It was time to hurriedly have our scarves blessed and say our goodbyes. Trekking with children can be guaranteed to enhance the experience in unforeseen ways.

After training in anthropology and medicine, **Matthew Ellis** practised and raised his family in Nepal. He co-authored Bradt's e-book *Your Child Abroad: a Travel Health Guide*. After 30 years in the UK National Health Service he became a Senior Lecturer in global child health, again working in Nepal. He combined his latest passions (olive-farming and cycling) by pedalling from Bristol to Greece – which will appear in a forthcoming book, provisionally entitled *The Cycle of Life*. Harriet is now studying Humanitarian Medicine in Liverpool.

Cycling in Mauritius
Hallam and Carole Murray

Before setting off from England in late 1993, we had almost been warned off Mauritius by a newspaper article. 'If you're not into sun, sea, sand and snorkelling,' the sceptical journalist maintained, you should expect only 'terminal boredom' from the country. Whilst our cycling adventure across this volcanic island in the Indian Ocean (twelve hundred miles off Africa) occasionally risked being terminal, not once was boredom on the agenda. Not with three-year-old Quin on the back of a bike.

The centre of Mauritius is dominated by dramatic jagged peaks, its coast by coral reefs, estuaries and a turquoise sea. Bright green sugar cane grows from rusty-red soil between piles of black volcanic boulders from which sprout tall chimneys, relics from the early days of sugar processing. (On our return, seeing a brick chimney in a field near Bath, Quin cried out: 'Look, sugar cane!') Crimson bottlebrush trees were blooming, so too purple lotus and cacti in multifarious colours. The ground was routinely covered with floral confetti and, appropriately, it was a wedding invitation that had lured us to this tropical island. But we couldn't travel all that way without a spot of adventure. The first-ever circumnavigation of the island by bicycle with toddler was there for the taking. No matter that we would be undertaking the expedition during the hottest months of the year as well as in cyclone season. What could possibly go wrong?

Our first base, in the capital of Port Louis, was in the half-built, cockroach-infested breeze-block home of a large Muslim family. On the first night in our extremely hot and airless, bare-concrete room, without so much as a hook on the wall or glass in the window, we struggled to sleep while sharing a single lumpy, horsehair mattress, with dogs barking, cats caterwauling, doors slamming and music blaring all around, until Quin pleaded, 'Can't we go home now?' We had some sympathy with his view.

The following day, Quin was scampering around steep, derelict land with the sparsely clothed young grandchildren of our host Satar, who made his living by selling sweets made of boiling sugar and coconut oil, cooked up in a huge cauldron perched precariously at waist height. One stumble on the attached cables would send this murderous liquid all over Quin or his new friends. This was just one of the hazards that confronted us wherever we went. Rarely did balconies, roofs or stairways (usually open to the elements) have any form of protection. Flat roofs littered with perilous detritus formed the main play areas, where obstacles routinely included vicious rusty steel rods protruding at uneven heights and unexpected angles. The dangers to Quin were magnified by the language barrier. The local children would call out a warning in Creole – 'watch out for the truck!' – but an uncomprehending Quin would continue building his castle of broken glass and tins in the middle of the street.

Satar and his family were very hospitable, but we yearned to get away from Port Louis and begin our real adventure. In a bazaar we bartered for two Taiwanese mountain bikes, to one of which we attached Quin's bike seat. Sale completed, our vendors announced:

'But you can't do it!' Baffled, we were taken to the colonial police headquarters, where the Chief of Police confirmed that it was indeed illegal to carry a child on a bicycle.

After a fruitless two days of queuing and negotiating (including with the Minister of Transport) in desperation, we again pleaded with the Chief of Police, who eventually winked his tacit approval. 'Just don't quote me,' he said. Luckily we needn't have worried, for once away from the capital we were in a different world, with village police greeting us warmly, not batting an eyelid about our travelling arrangements.

Attaching tent, mosquito net and Quin to one bike, and stuffing three peoples' worth of clothing and equipment into two panniers on the other, we felt terribly unsure of ourselves. Given the uncertain strength of our bikes, would we even survive the first day? But within a couple of hours, the noise and traffic of Port Louis were receding into our memories as we followed a winding earth road north, basking in our new-found freedom. From the comfort of his bike seat, Quin eagerly pointed out lizards, shrews and giant snails crossing the road. Bright yellow weaver birds bickered at nests dangling like unkempt beards from the tips of branches.

After three scorching days, we were well into our stride. Then came rumours of a cyclone. This unnerved Quin, who asked nervously: 'We wouldn't cycle in a cycland, would we?' Our uncertainty grew at the realisation that the sea was now eerily devoid of fishing boats. As the wind strengthened, cycling became difficult and we realised that camping too was out of the question. Battling on, we reached the village of Poudre D'Or, hoping for a place to stay, but the residents all shook their heads. The nearest accommodation was in a town we had passed two days earlier.

In desperation, we took shelter in a half-built 'villa' by a mangrove-filled lagoon. With the sun blotted out, lashing rain, sheet lightening and wind sufficiently fierce to bend tall palm trees almost horizontal, we swiftly became incredibly cold and damp. We had no warm clothing, no electricity and no clean water. Worse, we knew that cyclones could last a fortnight – and we were due back in Port Louis for the wedding by then. It was soon pitch dark and we were mesmerised by the noise and thrashing motion of palms against glimpses of the full, serene moon. Effectively imprisoned, we patched up the missing window panes with pannier supports and gaffer tape, put on every stitch of clothing and tried to stay cheerful.

Fortunately, the cyclone abated after two days, so we rejoined the road. We passed herds of primitive-looking horned cattle enclosed by lava-boulder walls or cactus fences. We crossed a swollen river where women were pounding clothes against the rocks and turning them into a patchwork of colour. In town and countryside alike we noticed that women tended to work all day long, whilst men gathered in the shade, smoking, drinking and playing Chinese dominoes.

Many think of Mauritius as an ideal holiday destination. However, facilities for independent travel were few, and tourism transpired to be concentrated in pockets around the golden beaches along the north and west coasts. Heat-cracked, potholed and corrugated roads made for slow progress – even more so post-cyclone, for they were strewn with all manner of oddly shaped seedpods and other debris. The south and east of the island were particularly tough going: sparsely populated, with steep cliffs dropping straight into mighty breakers. With every square inch of flat terrain cultivated or inhabited, there was often nowhere to camp. We moved on almost every day, eventually prompting a bemused and exhausted Quin to ask: 'Which home is it tonight?' Late one evening, after a tiring ride of twenty-odd miles, we took refuge in a crab-fisherman's hut. With no way of suspending our mosquito net, the giant, rampant mosquitoes were not the slightest bit deterred by the repellent drenching all three of us.

Mosquitoes were not the only wildlife with which we shared our life. Whether confronted by enormous spiders, evil-looking hornets or electric-blue flying beetles, Quin always seemed fascinated rather than frightened. He befriended one tiny frog and an entire family of cockroaches, letting them climb up and down his arms. He got the giggles when one landed on a menu, appearing to point out a favourite dish with its antennae!

As Christmas approached, we arrived at the historic port of Mahebourg and established a base in a clean, airy convent. In the courtyard was a stage, festooned with palm fronds. That night we were treated to a Nativity play, complete with real animals. By some kind of premonition Quin became perturbed. 'Baby Jesus is in danger,' he insisted repeatedly. And so he was, for just before the end the whole stage collapsed – fortunately without causing serious injury.

The following day, Christmas Eve, the convent closed and we set off again, a nun observing that we were 'like Mary and Joseph, with nowhere to stay'. We reached Souillac and tuned in to a few indistinct carols from Kings College, Cambridge, whilst awaiting the magical candlelit Catholic service. We camped under casuarinas on a beach of volcanic sand, looking up at the Southern Cross. (Father Christmas came a little late that year, only catching up with Quin once we returned to Port Louis. He had to come equipped with anti-ant chalk to keep the insatiable six-legged wretches out of the gingerbread man until morning. The residual chalk silhouette of a stocking on the floor next day looked like some macabre 'scene of the crime'!)

Travelling on to the west, we sought solace from the fierce midday heat under a group of strongly scented frangipani trees in the middle of nowhere. When Quin appeared carrying part of a skull, it dawned on us that we were resting in a Hindu cremation ground. On the last leg of our journey, we turned back to the north, continuing to hug the coast. We watched fishermen wading out into the sea, casting their nets in biblical fashion. Inspired, Quin sat on a rock, dangling a bamboo stick and string towards tropical fish swimming in the shallows. '*Croissants!*' he yelled, excitedly. ('*Poissons,*' we realised – fish.)

On New Year's Eve, the final day of our expedition, firecrackers, rowdy street markets and deafening music greeted our safe return to Port Louis. Celebrations continued with the wedding, where we all feasted from a large cauldron on the beach.

We lasted barely forty-eight hours in the capital before escaping once again. We headed to the headquarters of the Mauritius Wildlife Fund, to donate our bicycles. This charity arrived three centuries too late to save the dodo, but within a very few years it had rescued two other birds – Mauritius kestrel and pink pigeon – from the brink of extinction. Our last few nights were spent surrounded by passionate naturalists and their menagerie. Even our bed was strewn with glass tanks containing tarantulas and the eggs of rare lizards.

Our last excursion was a long hike up a deep gorge to locate a pair of the rare kestrels recently released into the wild. They swooped down from the trees to snatch dead white mice from Quin's hand. As evening approached, the chirping of cicadas and the croaking of bulbous-throated frogs provided the rainforest soundtrack as huge fruit bats glided silently between banyan trees. It couldn't have been further from terminal boredom.

Hallam Murray spent fifteen years in book publishing. He is now a freelance lecturer and photographer. He has travelled in over 40 countries, but his passion is for Latin America. Amongst many adventures, he cycled from California to Tierra del Fuego, visiting many inaccessible potter communities *en route*.

Carole Murray is a Fine Art Conservator, accomplished photographer and artist, exhibiting several works at the RA Summer Exhibition. In 1995 she won an award for a watercolour of Bangladesh at the Royal Society of Watercolours. She is an independent mental health campaigner and in 2018 contributed to the Independent Review of the Mental Health Act.

SCRAPES AND MISHAPS

Early Birds

Adrian Phillips

'I smoke a pipe, young lady,' I heard the elderly gentleman answer. 'That's why my teeth are black.'

I hurried across the restaurant and, with a red-faced apology, ushered Twin 1 back to our table. My wife was just returning from the washroom where she'd been mopping up Twin 2. 'It went everywhere,' she muttered. 'Even in his pants.'

Our table was a battlefield, scattered with the meal's casualties. We plonked Twins 1 and 2 back in front of pieces of paper smeared with peas and stuck down with crushed carrot, and they continued scrawling rainbows and eating the ends of their crayons. The airport was heaving. Fog had descended over the runway, delaying a string of flights, and the rows of plastic seats on the concourse were now full of bored passengers staring into space or sending exasperated texts. Those without seats perched uncomfortably on their carry-on luggage, or paced back and forth with tickets in hand, as if a demonstration of industriousness would somehow encourage the weather to push off elsewhere.

But *we* had a table. *We* had arrived well in advance of the fog – indeed, while the air was so clear and blue you could have dived right in. We'd breezed through security and staked out a spot in the restaurant three hours before our flight was scheduled to leave. Yes, welcome to Benny's Diner, smug city.

In truth, this was down to my wife Monika rather than me. She's one of those rise-early-and-get-everywhere-well-ahead-of-time types. By contrast, I tend to live my life in last-minute mode, dashing for trains and panting into meetings. The only subject on which we regularly disagree is the time we should leave the house to travel to mutual engagements. Monika likes to allow for potential obstacles along the way, anticipating traffic jams and breakdowns and rockfalls and baby deer lying injured in the road. It's such a gloomy view. 'You're a travel pessimist,' I tell her. 'You're a pain in the arse,' she tells me. And, discussion closed, we leave when she wants to leave.

Her one concession on this occasion, albeit offered reluctantly, was that while the fog was hunkering down we could remain in Benny's Diner even after the departures board read *Go to Gate 5*. 'The kids are far happier here, love,' I pointed out, trying to catch the waiter's eye to order another beer. 'It's only five minutes to the gate. If we wait until it says *Boarding* we'll still have plenty of time to get there and join the queue.' Monika looked anxious. 'Listen, everyone knows the airlines put these things up on the board far earlier than they need to,' I said, standing my ground, and digging into my second pudding.

The fog was fading at last and – a full hour after our original departure time had passed – the sign changed to *Boarding*. 'Hooray,' I said cheerfully, wiping my mouth on the napkin. 'Time to mosey on over to the gate. Anybody need the loo?' But the sign hadn't finished. The letters fluttered and clattered once more, and, when they stopped, the word *Boarding* had disappeared and *Final Call* had taken its place. Welcome to Benny's Diner, panic city.

'I *told* you!' hissed Monika as she swept crayons and dinosaurs and wet wipes and crumbs and stray bits of sausage from the table into her bag. But now wasn't the time for recriminations. Now was the time to grab a twin by the hand and hotfoot it to the gate.

Unless you've had to rush to meet an airline's final call with four-year-olds in tow, you can't fully appreciate how short their legs are. I was well into my stride before I realised that Twin 2 was dragging behind me on his stomach like a waterskier who'd taken a tumble but forgotten to let go of the rope.

'Come on, quick, quick!' I said, stopping briefly to heave him up in my left arm before continuing the chase. His head was now next to my ear, which suited him far better because he could ask me all the questions he needed answering about the current situation.

'Yes, we have to run to catch the plane,' I huffed. 'Yes, you are heavy,' I puffed. 'Yes, the bag is heavy too… Yes, even though it's on wheels,' I wheezed.

I slalomed through an endless crowd of people who seemed to be taking part in some sort of slow-walking competition.

'… I've no idea whether the pilot has finished his lunch… No, he's not angry with us… Yes, I think mummy might be a bit angry with me… No, she's not a faster runner than me – it's just that her bag is lighter… Yes, I'm sure my face is going red… No, Peppa Pig won't be on the plane… No, I can't drive a plane… Well, bully for Miss Rabbit…'

I don't know whether Usain Bolt has ever run between Benny's Diner and Gate 5 burdened with a wheelie case and an inquisitive child, but if he has then I bet he didn't do it much quicker than me. But it wasn't quick enough. My wife was already at the gate (her bag was definitely lighter than mine), and her expression told the story. Gate closed. 'I TOLD YOU WE SHOULD HAVE GONE TO THE GATE EARLIER!' she thundered. Clearly *now* was the time for recriminations. 'You're ALWAYS leaving things last minute and it's 9 p.m. and what will we do about the hotel and the hire car and the kids and what are we going to do?!'

'Errrm' was all I could muster as I bent over, hands on knees, gasping like a beached fish.

Once I'd gathered enough oxygen to speak, I decided to plead our case to the remaining representative of the airline standing at the gate. But the representative of the airline (which, to preserve its anonymity, I'll call Iron Stare) was not a person to be pleaded with.

'You are advised to arrive at the airport in good time for your flight, sir,' said the representative of Iron Stare.

'We were here four hours early,' I countered. 'There must have been something wrong with the board.'

'In good time for your flight, sir,' she continued, as if I'd not spoken. 'Our website makes it very clear, sir. Very clear.' And then she stood stock-still and silent, gazing blank-eyed at a point somewhere above my head, like a robot on standby.

'Well, what now?' I asked glumly. 'We've two young kids.'

'Once your luggage has been removed from the hold, it can be collected from the carousel in arrivals,' she resumed, rebooting herself briefly. 'You can get there through the door next to Sunglasses Palace.' Then she powered down for the night.

The door next to Sunglasses Palace turned out to be invisible. Of course it did. We walked back and forth and roundabout, looking one side and the other, and even around the back. It was 10.30 p.m. before a washroom attendant took pity on us and showed us a door that wasn't invisible next to a different place called Sunglasses Shack. Through the door, we joined a gaggle of miserable miscreants who'd also missed their flights, before our passports were checked and we were ejected through another door.

The definition of travel purgatory is queuing to drop off your luggage and then queuing to collect your luggage without enjoying a holiday in between. It was made worse by having to stand in a throng of suntanned holidaymakers returning from the place we were meant now to be jetting towards. The kids were happy enough, of course; for kids, there's no better playground than a luggage carousel. 'Don't do that, Twin 1!' called Monika. 'No! Mind your fingers!'

I decided to take control by slipping away in search of someone who might rebook us seats on the next available flight, and perhaps offer a sympathetic ear to my complaints about the departures board next to Benny's Diner. Unfortunately, Twin 2 thought I should have some company.

'No, we won't be at the airport for ever and ever,' I answered as she trotted alongside me. 'No, the pilot hasn't stolen our bags… No, you can't have an ice cream… Yes, I know you're being good, but it's 11 p.m. and there's no ice-cream shop open… Yes, I wish we could do magic too… Probably chocolate and caramel.'

A queue five miles long zigzagged back and forth in front of the Iron Stare customer services desk. There was a solitary member of staff on duty, as glassy-eyed as his colleague I'd met earlier. I abandoned hope, but joined the line anyway because, well, anything was better than the carousel. And while I queued, I logged on to the Iron Stare website. There was another flight at 6.30 a.m. the following day. I entered our details, unticked boxes adding insurance and priority boarding and other things I didn't want, and pressed confirm. The website informed me I had failed to complete a compulsory field. After much scrolling, I tracked the problem down to the 'Title' field. The website required me to enter 'Mr', but it wouldn't let me enter 'Mr', and without me entering 'Mr' it wouldn't let me complete the booking. I could have wept.

But now wasn't the time for weeping. Now was the time to phone a friend, wake him from his slumber, urge him out of bed, listen to him playing the martyr as he trudged downstairs in his dressing gown, and talk him through the booking on his home computer. Success! Despite moving just five yards in the last half hour, we'd taken a giant stride towards our holiday. I scooped up Twin 2 (who was busy trying to peel second-hand chewing gum from the floor), bade a silent farewell to the suckers in the queue for customer services, and returned to the queue for our luggage and then the queue for a crowded shuttle bus transferring passengers to queues at various hotels.

As the bus rumbled along, Monika checked the websites of the hotels on the route. Fully booked. Fully booked. Each fully booked with passengers whose flights had been cancelled because of the earlier fog.

'Yes, it's just like in the Bible, Twin 1,' I replied mechanically. 'No, we won't have to sleep with the sheeps, Twin 2,' I said dully.

However, miracle of miracles, it seemed there might be room at the final inn. We were the only passengers who'd travelled this far, the very last to disgorge. It was 1 a.m. when we dinged a little bell at reception that summoned a man so irritatingly cheerful that I wanted to punch him in the face.

'How are you doing this evening – ah, sorry, this *morning*?' he asked chirpily, as he tapped away at his computer. 'Off on your hols?'

'We believe you have a room,' I said.

'Yes, indeed! This is your lucky day!'

'Quite. Just what we were thinking,' I muttered as he continued tapping and smiling. But then a frown crossed the face of this grown-up Pollyanna. 'We have a problem, Houston,' he said. 'I'm afraid you're a family. And this isn't a family room.'

Now was the time for weeping. Monika's eyes filled, and she launched our story at the poor man. She told him how organised she'd been, and how stupid I'd been, and how good the kids had been, all things considered. She talked of a sprint to the gate, of stony-souled airline staff, of a carousel and a crowded bus, and she repeated how stupid I'd been, just in case he'd missed the point first time round. I stood by her side, nodding dumbly. As she stifled a sob and prepared to issue forth a fresh barrage of woe, the man pushed a room card across the counter and beat a hasty retreat.

There were no baths or bedtime stories. Twins 1 and 2 were out for the count, their heads lolling over our shoulders as we hauled ourselves up to the room. We folded them into one of the twin beds, and we squeezed into the other.

'Right, so the flight leaves in just over five hours,' I said, looking at my watch. 'What time shall I set the alarm for?'

'For two hours' time.'

'*What?* We're only half an hour from the airport. You're such a travel pessimist.'

'And you're a pain in the arse.'

Adrian Phillips is MD of Bradt, and a writer/broadcaster who contributes to media including *The Telegraph*, *National Geographic*, the BBC and ITV. He is currently the British Guild of Travel Writers 'Travel Writer of the Year', the Travel Media 'Consumer Writer of the Year', and Latin American Travel Association 'Magazine Writer of the Year'. He tweets at @adrianphillips1.

The Husky Ride

Maria Pieri

'Keep your feet on the brake when you stop, or the huskies will go.' Check.

'If you take your feet off the sledge, the huskies will go.' Check.

'If you stop, you have to keep both feet on the brake, or the huskies will go. To turn left, lean left. For right, lean right. Do not take your feet off the sledge. If you do, you will find the huskies will go.'

Check. And check. Sure, I've got all that.

These are the instructions to the group of six families being delivered by Lionel, our hard-core husky entrepreneur at the snowy Wild Arctic Husky Park, located just a few hundred metres from the entrance of the Ranua Wildlife Park in Finland. He is the epitome of the active outdoorsy Scandi: rugged, bearded, red-nosed, unflappable.

Unlike me. I've 'driven' a husky sledge before but that was solo and felt a lot less pressured. Today I've got my two children with me, aged nine and seven; too young to assist, yet prematurely full of teenage angst and teenage opinions.

'Are you sure you can do this?' asks my son.

Dad's back in the UK and I've elected to take them on a winter adventure in Finnish Lapland to meet Santa in a slightly less commercial setting than the well-known Rovaniemi Santa Park. The husky ride is part of a magical Lapland experience combining the kids' love of snow and huskies – they're in the midst of a TY soft-toy fad and huskies are the cuddly toy of the moment. Meeting one in real life? That's parent brownie points worth having.

Everyone readies and sets off, although I'm the only one of the group without an adult partner. Our team of four huskies is watching all the sledges head off – I'm one from the back and the two guides are up ahead – and the dogs are agitated, tugging at the reins.

'Keep the huskies in the order assigned,' Lionel's words echo round my head. 'Don't let them overtake one another, they know what they're doing, and they work as a pack.'

Easier said than done as I realise I'm physically trying to hold them back.

Firstly we're overtaken by another family trying to get the hang of the 'controls'. I let them go ahead, despite some protesting from the kids, but in the process have to brake sharper than I'd like, or in fact the huskies like. One husky has taken issue with his teammate and the reins become entangled, until the husky is literally underneath the sledge.

The kids are beginning to panic, and I'm trying to reassure them everything will be fine. But I can't step off the brake or help at all.

'It's going to die,' says my daughter, always one for melodrama. 'Can you get the sledge off the husky?'

I can't. *'If you take your feet off the sledge, the huskies will go.'*

And to top it all off, the huskies are, erm, having a tiff.

'Muuuummm, they're trying to bite one another,' says my daughter on the verge of hysterics, setting her brother off into a crying whimper.

After some shouting from the sledge in front, one of the guides returns and untangles the huskies. My kids are looking on in disbelief, teary and scared.

'Do, the dogs get on?' I ask. Yes of course, our guide reassures us.

After some further calming (kids and dogs) we set off.

Then we have to stop again. There's been a crash. Ahead between the trees and ferns we can see a well-nourished family has overturned their sledge on one of the turns. They have to be assisted up and back onto the track.

Then we stop again.

'Now what?' says my daughter, full of bravado since we've had a clean run with the huskies and we're no longer the ones causing problems.

Another family – our British friends in fact – have hit a fir tree. No injuries, but they've just had to be helped back up.

Then we stop again. We're not sure why this time. The yelling suggests it's another incident. We began this illuminated one-hour husky safari at 4 p.m. and by this point I'm willing this to end, the kids are complaining of the cold and failing light, and we're all hoping our team are not the ones to cause further distress.

The dogs have other ideas, resolving to continue their spat, reaching across from time to time to snarl at one another. As we reach the penultimate ridge, they get tangled up again.

I've had to pretty much brake the whole way to prevent the dogs catching up with the other sledges – they do not like being at the back – and its physically exerting.

Argh. And I still can't step off the sledge.

'Mum, it's really getting dark,' says my daughter fearfully.

'Don't worry, someone will come.' A little later someone eventually did.

Tired and a little shaken up we finally return to camp and the kids can't wait to get out of the sledge. One of the dog handlers helps uncouple dogs from sledge as I briefly retell our experience to explain why they kids are backing away from the dogs.

'Oh no, these two dogs don't really get on,' says one of the handlers.

Argh, again. 'I knew it,' says my daughter. 'We said that,' added my son, beating an even faster retreat from the dogs.

The website blurb says you have the chance of seeing hard-running, cheerily barking husky dogs which you can pet. My kids didn't want to pet the dogs and the huskies have fallen low on their list of eulogised stuffed toys – instead they've been compartmentalised as scary, real-life animals, along with all dogs. No brownie points for mum.

Luckily, we're meeting Santa tomorrow. We've still got sledging and snow angels to do and make, and 24 hours from now, I've still got a hole to fall down, which they will find hilarious. My daughter will also find and meet a new favourite animal to replace the husky – the Arctic fox at the wildlife centre will even accompany us back home in all its different incarnations and motifs, from stuffed toys to illustrated pencil cases.

Still, a note to Lionel (who did look broken, but is still in business; I checked): I did not take my feet off the brake. But huskies really do 'go'.

Maria Pieri is the Editorial Director for National Geographic Traveller (UK), with over 20 years' experience in creating award-winning content across all mediums. Just as challenging is being a mum of two almost-teen  children (if not in age, in attitude), both of whom share her love of travel, storytelling and Taekwondo.

The Night I Took My Daughters to a Filipino Brothel

Hugh Brune

It's true. I did. My two daughters, aged 16 and 14, spent the night in a brothel with their parents. But before you call the authorities I offer four mitigating pleas in my defence. First, I have only the word of my brother, who had got us into this fine mess, that our accommodation was actually a brothel: it may genuinely have been a 'karaoke hotel' as the sign outside claimed (which would explain why they rented rooms by the hour, right?). Second, as far as we could tell, there was no business going on that evening (no karaoke either, mercifully). Third, this was an unplanned stop and a last resort. Finally, and most importantly, I think we all learned something from the experience. In retrospect, I have no regrets. Let me tell you how it happened.

* * *

The Filipino custom of *bayanihan* has no direct equivalent in English. Roughly it means 'co-operation by a group or community to achieve a particular task'. Originally referring to the tradition of villagers helping a neighbour move house by physically picking up the building using wooden poles and carrying it to a new location, now it can be applied to any scenario where a community comes together to solve a problem. But, like any untranslatable foreign word, you really have to see it in action to understand it. One way to see the practice – not necessarily recommended – is to do what we did. Drive a wreck of a hire car from Bangued to Tabui on the island of Luzon. Do so along a mountain road clearly fit for four-wheel drives only. Break down. Get rescued by a truckful of labourers who simply refuse to leave until they have helped you out. Then stand back and watch the show.

What were we doing on this manifestly unsuitable stretch of road? Ask my brother. He was navigating. Admittedly, the route looked fine on the map, and up to a few miles beyond the village of Lagangilang it *was* fine – a perfectly normal paved road. Thereafter it became a dirt track – riddled with rocks, holes and puddles – skimming sheer drops down to the valley. Driving in two cars (one with my brother and his partner; the other with my wife, daughters and me), we were trying to get from Vigan to the famous rice terraces of Banaue, and by now were chasing the sunk-cost fallacy. Having committed to this route over the mountains, it was too late to turn back, take the long way round and still make Banaue before dark.

So we pressed on in the fading hope that the paved road would miraculously return. We bumped and scraped for four miles or so before there was a final, fatal crunch underneath us and the car refused to move further. In the forty-five minutes it had taken us to drive the short distance we had seen no other vehicles. My brother and his partner were ahead of us, now out of sight. We had no phone signal. If we hadn't had kids in the car, I'd have happily said – and said loudly and firmly – that we were fucked.

I went through the motions of lifting the bonnet and peering inside, although to nobody's surprise I failed to identify the problem, let alone fix it. My wife and I made some quick calculations. It was the middle of the day; the sun would set around six. If by four o'clock we hadn't found some way out of this situation we would walk back to Lagangilang and throw ourselves at the mercy of the friendly-looking villagers. We thought that having a plan would reassure our suddenly pale and silent children, but it didn't seem to.

Two jeeps did now pass us in quick succession. Both drivers stopped and asked if we were OK. Both said they would report our situation in Lagangilang and ask the villagers to send up a mechanic. This offered a flicker of hope. Then my brother and his partner arrived. They had finally given up on the road a few miles further on and turned back unilaterally. My brother appraised the situation carefully.

'Yup,' he said, 'we're fucked.'

The children didn't laugh at hearing a grown-up swear.

And then, like a mirage, the trucks appeared. They stopped and men eager to help poured out. There was no argument; it was immediately clear they weren't going to move on until they had rescued us, however long it took. There wasn't an expert among them, but they had unswerving confidence in their ability as a group to help us out. They surrounded the stalled vehicle. They rolled it down to the nearest stretch of flat-ish road. A group of them lifted the car while another peered under the front wheel. He came out nodding and smiling.

My brother's partner, translating, said the group had found the fault. They couldn't fix it here but would help us move the car back to the village where we would be able to find a mechanic. So, very carefully and slowly, a dozen of us wheeled the car back over the holes, through the puddles, around the sheer drops. When we reached the top of the paved road, one of the men leaped into the driver's seat and freewheeled through the twists and turns all the way down to Lagangilang, his echoing whoops bouncing around the valley.

It was nearly two hours from when the group of men first stopped to when they left our car, still broken, safely by the road back in civilisation. None of them had phones so were unable to warn their families that they were going to be late home. And we didn't even get to say goodbye, let alone thank them properly. While the villagers were bringing out drinks for the children, and I was discussing with my brother what an appropriate tip might be, our saviours vanished back into their trucks and sped away. We ran after them, waving and calling out our gratitude.

Bayanihan.

Six of us, with our luggage, then wedged ourselves into my brother's car. We drove to the next village where we were told we would find the region's sole car mechanic. He was waiting for us at the garage, which doubled as a bar, grocery store and all-purpose community hub. We told him where we had left the car and he went off on his moped, back the way we had come, to look at it. While he was gone, we asked around after places to stay. The nearest place turned out to be in a town a further half-hour along the road. So we decided that my brother would go and check us into the hotel while we waited for news from the mechanic. He'd then drive back and pick us up.

It had grown dark by now. We sat outside the garage, and I rang the hotel in Banaue to tell them that we wouldn't be making our reservation. We bought snacks and drinks but were too exhausted to eat them. A television balanced on crates showed *The Voice of the*

Philippines, a raucous local version of the popular talent show. Next to it, a long cage of live chickens did a brisk trade. A moped would pull up, the rider would hand over some notes, then roar off with a squawking bird under his arm.

Younger Daughter asked: 'What if the hotel is full?'

We assured her that this was unlikely, but that if it was, we'd find somewhere else. For my wife and me, now the immediate danger was over, the adventure had a whiff of nostalgia about it. This is how we used to travel, we told our children. When we were your age (immediate eye-rolling from the teenagers), you couldn't plan everything in advance. You couldn't wade through shrill reviews on TripAdvisor, or post a query on Thorn Tree, or email a range of hotels with your special requirements. Instead, you'd pitch up somewhere and ask around. It's OK, we said, we've done this before. The girls didn't look convinced. (It didn't seem prudent to mention that occasionally this strategy would lead to sleeping in train stations or on beaches, although I noted privately that at least the air was warm here, down off the mountain, and it wasn't raining. If the worst came to the worst...)

After an hour or so, the mechanic returned. He would be able to get the part we needed tomorrow, he told us. He would go back up when it was light, tow our car to the garage and fix it here. It would be ready for us by the end of the day. Of the various scenarios playing out in our heads this was by some distance the best. We thanked him, greatly relieved. Then my brother showed up. He'd found the hotel and secured us rooms. Although, he warned, 'it's not ideal.'

'What do you mean, not ideal?'

'You'll see.'

So we crammed back into his car and drove to the hotel. 'First clue,' he said as we arrived. 'The car park's round the back.' Then he showed us a sign: '*Air-conditioned private rooms, ₱150 per hour*'.

Look, it wasn't the worst place I've stayed in. It was clean. Ish. It was quiet: it was evidently off-season, so there were neither squeaking mattresses nor screeching karaoke machines. I think there was just one other person staying there. It was cheap. The woman at the desk was friendly. There was a picture of Jesus on the wall. Best of all, it was open.

But Elder Daughter had overheard our mutterings and twigged where we were. 'This is a brothel,' she said, 'isn't it? You've brought us to stay in a brothel.'

'No,' I said, 'it's a karaoke hotel,' and pointed to the colourful sign that encouraged us to '*SING ALL YOU CAN!*'

We slept fitfully in rooms that had just a few too many mirrors on the wall. The following day we returned to the garage, collected our car and continued with our holiday.

* * *

And the lessons for my children? Well, not to trust their uncle with a map again, obviously. That, just occasionally, it's OK not to know at eight o'clock in the evening where you'll be sleeping that night. Travel, to paraphrase John Lennon, is what happens when you're making other plans. But mainly this – and it's a delicate message for a parent to convey:

Stay out of trouble, girls. No, seriously. You don't want to be a headline. This episode on the mountain, easily avoidable with the tiniest shred of common sense, could have ended badly. The men in the trucks could have robbed and beaten us up, or worse. We were idiots. But if, despite the extravagant precautions you're going to take, you do end up in a jam, remember what happened and know this: *the odds are still in your favour*. Because those men weren't bandits. They were patient and helpful and good-humoured, and they didn't even need to be thanked at the end of it. As well as being a beautiful thing to behold, *bayanihan* is, it seems, its own reward.

Hugh Brune is head of sales and marketing at Bradt Travel Guides. He is the author of two published novels as well as a few unpublished ones, and has also written for television, film and the theatre. His two daughters have now safely left home and are responsible for their own travel arrangements.

The Best Medicine

Vernon Lacey

Steffi turns and looks to me for confirmation: 'Josy's with you, right?' It's a look that's been part of our parent repertoire for a long time. I know it well.

Only this time Josy, our three-year-old, is not with me.

I drop to my knees to look for her. Through a thicket of legs I can see Steffi's distinctive blue shoes several metres away. But no Josy. No girl with brown hair. No red jacket.

Panic shoots through me like an electric shock.

When I stand up I find Steffi's expectant eyes. I raise a hand above the heads and point a forefinger towards her. 'She went your way,' I indicate, thinking Josy's got ahead of her mum.

It's the height of summer, our first visit to Cornwall's Eden Project, and the walkway through the tropical rainforest biome is busy. 'Josy! Josy!' I call out, sidestepping visitors and looking around.

I hear Steffi's voice drawing near. 'Josy… Josy…' she's saying in a reassuring yet pleading way.

A moment later we're facing one another.

'Where is she?' Steffi asks.

I feel stricken.

The disappearance invokes a terrifying thought. 'I thought she was with you.'

'Josy,' Steffi calls out, turning her head.

We kneel. Look frantically around. Stand.

No child.

'Let's double back,' Steffi says. 'Either she has got ahead of me on the walkway or she's somewhere back towards the entrance.'

Steffi's cool logic galvanises me. 'You're right,' I say. 'She can't get out of the biome alone. It's enclosed.'

'Keep your phone in your hand,' Steffi says, looking around. 'Whoever finds her first rings the other.'

For a fleeting moment our eyes meet again. I'm fighting a terror within. I know Steffi is too, but her look is resolute.

She turns and is gone, and I double back along the walkway.

Moving against the prevailing direction of travel, I am forced to dodge visitors, appealing to my child as I make my way: 'Josy...'

Visitors glance around. One man puts his hand on the shoulder of a young boy. From a distance Steffi's entreaties – 'Josy! Josy! Come to mama!' – hang menacingly in the air.

Not minutes earlier the diversity of the biome, housing the biggest artificial rainforest on earth, was a magical place: leaves the size of elephants' ears, fluorescent flowers, bananas and the music of a cascading waterfall. 'Are we really going to South America?' Josy had asked with eyes wide open when we entered.

Now the rainforest is a place of shadows, darkness and danger.

My heart is thumping. 'Josy! Josy!' I bawl.

I look this way. That way. It feels like the domed roof is a web trapping me. Palm fronds jab. The waterfall gurgles monstrously. Bamboo stems thrust upwards. Exposed roots are skeletal. And the African totems huddled together, the colour of obsidian, glare with secretive, cavernous eyes.

'Josy! Josy!' I holler.

On the Rainforest Aerial Walkway there is finally space to move freely. I make my way across, looking everywhere for my child. Scanning the thick undergrowth below.

Suddenly I see a girl in a red top.

'JOSY!'

The girl stops. Turns. But it isn't my child.

The girl points at the biome roof. 'Like a big honeycomb,' she says of its luminescent hexagonal segments. The adult with her looks up. Smiling.

I put my hands on a railing and look across the complex. Steffi's piercing petitions – 'J… o… s…y… Where are you?' – ride the cloying air.

I'm palpitating. I don't know myself like this. The enormity of the search has hit me full force. I look at my phone. There is no call. No message. We are visitors to England. We live in Germany. We haven't activated our telephone provider's calls-abroad option. The realisation exasperates me.

Alone on the bridge, fears accelerate. Josy's being led away… She's fallen in the pool… or under the waterfall… She's alone … afraid…

She needs us.

'She must be down there,' I tell myself, possessed with sudden determination. 'She must be. We're going to find her. We're going to find our Josy.'

On saying it a power surges from the darkness of tyrannical fear, and in an instant I'm subject to its will, spontaneously bellowing my child's name with guttural force: 'JO… SY! JO… SY!'

My outburst alerts visitors.

'Can I help?,' asks a man. His curious, concerned eyes peer from behind spectacles. 'Have you lost someone?'

My heart pounds as I blurt out: 'My child... My child... She's disappeared.'

'What is she wearing?' someone asks.

'How old is she?' Another voice.

'What's her name?' enquires a third person.

I look back and forth across the faces.

'We'll help you,' the man wearing glasses says. He looks at a young girl. She must be six or seven years old. Her green eyes are wide open. 'This is my daughter, Lizzie. She'll help, too.'

'Yes – please help me,' I implore. 'Red top – a jumper – brown hair. Beige trousers. Aged three. Her name's Josy – Josy Lacey.'

'I'll go to the staff,' one person says.

'I'll guard the entrance.'

'I'll go this way,' says another.

Suddenly a volunteer search party springs into action. There is purpose. Activity. The disappearance has taken on a whole new meaning. In place of isolating fear there is a connection with strangers.

I follow the start of the path that we took upon entering the biome. It is thick with visitors. Soon I'm at the point where Josy disappeared. 'JOSY! JOSY!' I utter determinedly.

By now ten agonising minutes have passed. I listen intently. No familiar voice calling our child. Has Steffi found her? Wherever Steffi is, our goal unites us.

I press on. We must find Josy, I tell myself. She must be in the biome. 'JOSY! JOSY!'

Someone is pulling at my arm. I turn. It's Lizzie's father. 'Come quickly...,' he says. 'I think we've found your daughter. Back this way. Just a few yards along here.'

He leads the way, twisting between the visitors.

Then stops and points across a rope cordon to Josy, sitting next to Lizzie.

The sudden shift in events overpowers me. 'JOSY!' I stammer, catching my breath. 'Come on out.'

Josy and Lizzie are several metres back from the walkway, sitting on the floor and partly concealed under the leaves of a large plant. Josy looks at me. She has a red pepper in her hand.

'Josy. Come on out now,' I appeal.

She's in no rush to come over. 'My daddy puts these on my favourite pizzas,' she says, turning back to Lizzie.

I'm on the walkway. My emotions are a sea of chaos. Panic and relief, fear and liberation tumble like waves, each taking the place of the one that goes before. I could not be more removed from the carefree children sitting on a piece of Cornish earth, surrounded by the invisible, protective cocoon of their innocence.

Steffi arrives and sees Josy. 'She's safe, she's safe…' Steffi pants as her body, like a runner crossing the finishing line, folds and her hands collapse on to her knees.

'And I like them a lot,' Josy says to Lizzie. 'They're delumptious.'

Steffi straightens herself and gives me a look that is half-agonised, half-euphoric, then turns again to the children. 'Josy… come to mama,' she urges from behind the rope cordon.

'Lizzie, come now,' the girl's father demands.

A gardener appears. 'I would give that to me,' she says as she lifts the cordon and strides towards the children. 'That's a very hot chilli pepper. It could burn your skin.'

Why didn't I twig? Josy thinks it's a sweet pepper. Steffi gives me a look with a new meaning. What should be a joyous reunion takes on new urgency.

'Don't bite it, Josy,' I implore, my voice still shaking. 'Give it to the woman.'

The gardener extends her hand. 'Give it to me,' she demands. The bright red pepper has evidently fallen off one of the plants. It must have caught Josy's attention so that she left the walkway to have a closer look at it.

'But it doesn't burn,' Josy says. She holds up the pepper and its glossy red skin reveals teeth marks.

The gardener looks around at us. 'We need to get her to the on-site doctor urgently,' she says. 'I'm worried. They're extremely hot peppers for a child.' Then, with a clinical sweep of her arm, she snatches the pepper from Josy's hand. Josy looks stunned. Her eyes are fixed on the gardener.

'How long ago did you bite it?' the woman asks Josy.

'Just before Lizzie came,' Josy says.

'And did Lizzie bite it too?' Lizzie shakes her head.

Josy scrambles to her feet and comes running into the arms of her mum. Her eyes are glossy.

The relief silences me. And it stills Steffi who embraces Josy as a drowning person would cling to a buoy. I stroke Josy's head. At close range I see her lips are swelling.

'Come… come,' the gardener says. 'It's urgent.'

'Can my friend Lizzie come?' Josy asks, lifting her head off Steffi's shoulder.

Lizzie's father looks at me.

'Let's all go together,' I say.

Steffi hugs Josy possessively. Caressing her. I see Josy's head from behind, bobbing up and down on Steffi's shoulder as we make our way. I want to hug her. Hold her. Nothing could mean more to a parent than finding a lost child. We should be celebrating. Not running to a doctor.

'My daughter can wait here,' Lizzie's father says when we arrive at the medical centre. 'I need to let the search party know that Josy's safe.'

'Search party?' Steffi says, looking at me.

'Yes. Indeed. Tell them that we're so grateful,' I say to Lizzie's father, realising I haven't thanked anyone yet.

The doctor enters just as Lizzie's dad leaves. Josy is still clinging monkey-like to her mum. Arms around her neck, legs around her waist.

Lizzie sits on a chair and fixes her eyes on Josy.

'What happened?' The doctor asks.

'She's bitten a chilli pepper,' I reply.

The doctor turns to Josy. 'Now what's your name?' he asks.

'Josy Lacey.'

'And how old are you, Josy?'

Josy starts to lisp several words. 'I'm a bit more than thwee.'

'And what happened exactly?'

'I saw a nice pepper lying on the floor,' she says. 'The ones my daddy puts on my favourwat pizza.'

'Did you really bite it?'

'Yes.'

'Do you have it with you?'

Josy shakes her head.

The gardener produces the pepper.

'Aha!' the doctor says, holding up the offending item. 'The famous red-hot chilli pepper. Spicy. But not poisonous.'

'Are you here on holiday?' the doctor asks Josy.

'Yeth,' Josy says. 'We've come fwom Munich. My mummy's German and my daddy's Englith. It's my firth time in England. Weef seen the rainfowest.'

Lizzie's smile is precious. Her father enters the consulting room just in time to see it.

'Open your mouth, Josy,' the doctor says.

She throws back her head and opens her mouth wide.

The doctor shines a clip torch inside. Then he presses Josy's lips gently together between his fingers. 'Nod if your lips are stinging,' he says.

Josy nods at the ceiling.

'Badly?' the doctor asks. Josy grunts and shakes her head.

'Now,' says the doctor, releasing Josy's lips. 'I've got the best medicine in Cornwall for you. Would you like to know what it is?'

'Yeth.'

'A big, delicious, cooling ice cream. Any flavour you like.'

Josy's eyes light up.

Lizzie's got her hands tucked under her thighs. She hunches her shoulders and turns to her dad with eyes full of laughter.

The doctor reads out the prescription as he writes it:

'Josy Lacey. Aged three and a bit. Ice cream after patient's liking. Three times a day for the rest of her holiday, if needed.'

'Can my friend Lizzie have one too?' Josy asks.

Vernon Lacey grew up in Cheshire, UK. He teaches English Literature and Philosophy and lives in Munich with his German wife and three children. His travel memoir *South to Barcelona* was published by Ant Press in 2018. His interests include cycling, guitar, and learning languages.

Returning

Elizabeth Pimm

'OK,' I said. 'You look after him. I'll be back in a week.'

I had flown from Perth in Western Australia to Kuala Lumpur (Malaysia) the previous day with my eleven-month-old son and an equally large and cumbersome stuffed koala bear that was too big to fit in a suitcase. It was daunting to be in sole charge, but my courageous husband was in northwest Australia digging a railway line to earn our fares back to Britain.

Three years earlier, when my then fiancé did not gain the place he wanted in a British university, we had the bright idea of trying our luck in Australia. We were both accepted for degree courses at the University of Western Australia. So, off we went – taking advantage of an offer to emigrate on a £10 fare. My fiancé went first to earn some money and find us a place to live. I followed a few months later. The early months were far from plain sailing, trying to study while earning enough money to live on. I swear that running past Perth Zoo in the early morning to get to work, even the kookaburras laughed at us.

But all things come to those who persevere. Within a few short years, we were married and we had a son, whose birthplace meant that he automatically became an Australian citizen – a state of affairs that would cause problems later... My husband graduated and was offered a post back in Britain. Our Australian adventure was over, although first we had to make it back home. With husband busy moving earth (if not heaven) to pay for our passage, my son and I set off together. The plan was to break the journey in Malaysia and then Pakistan, the latter to introduce my son – the first grandchild – to his paternal grandparents.

At the end of the first flight, my son and I stepped out of the cool atmosphere of the plane into what felt like a universal steam bath and were soon transported to a large hotel in downtown Kuala Lumpur. Our overheated little boy was tired and in unfamiliar surroundings. Understandably, he was howling in protest. A chambermaid came running in, picked him up and disappeared into the labyrinth of corridors and rooms. I was stupefied and rushed after her clutching a hotel robe around me.

One fruitless search later, I returned to my room in total panic. Kidnapped? Gone? What could I do? After an unbelievably fraught hour phoning reception, who were reluctant to get the police involved, and constantly ringing 'housekeeping', the woman returned with my beaming baby. 'He very happy now. Very beautiful boy. We went to kitchen to find some good food and everyone loved him. I come again if he cries.' He was indeed a beautiful, happy and contented little boy. His mother, in contrast, was washed out and faint with relief. I hugged my son tight and locked the door. Phase one of our journey home was complete.

The next day we arrived in Karachi for phase two (grandparents). At passport control, I handed over my documents, expecting easy passage. But after much discussion several officials were called over. Eventually my passport was returned to me. 'Sorry Madam, *you* can enter Pakistan... but not your *son*.' It transpired that being Australian came with a catch. Although my firstborn featured on my UK passport, a previously unseen note stipulated that he was not a 'Citizen of the United Kingdom and Colonies'. This meant that he could not enter Pakistan.

I paused then smiled sweetly at the uniformed men, sat my son down squarely on the broad counter with his koala and nappy bag and turned towards the exit. I asked the officials to look after my son for a week until I returned as I had really important meetings to attend which I couldn't cancel. I left a row of totally bemused faces and a smiling baby, happy to be the centre of attention. One of the uniforms caught up with me. 'No, no, Madam. You must take him with you, but this is most irregular.' By this time, we were all laughing.

A reprieve. Would baby, koala and I actually make it to Britain safely? I wondered what was coming next. It was certainly not proving easy to travel across the world with sole responsibility for two small but very important charges.

We drove north to Lahore and beyond, enjoying a few days climbing around the foothills of the Himalayas with the little one in a baby-carrier backpack shouldered by my brother-in-law who was also visiting. In such beautiful surroundings, it feels a betrayal to confess that I caught a stomach bug and rushed off at tangents at frequent intervals. Nevertheless, such indisposition offered one sure way of getting a different perspective on the world while remaining within earshot of my son's contented chatter.

For the last – airborne – stage of this epic mother-and-son journey we had a cot strapped onto the plane seat in front, at eye level. While my son slept, all was well. At other times, it was totally frustrating. Inevitably, my meal arrived before his, prompting the hungry child to reach for the food determinedly. Trying to keep him aloft and beyond arm's length proved trying and ultimately impossible. The airline's rule was that children should remain strapped in their designated place throughout the journey. Thank goodness that today's arrangements are so different.

After an eternity, we touched down at London Heathrow airport having just changed into clean clothes. I sighed with relief. It was the turn of my parents to meet their first grandchild. He would look fresh and cute, and their daughter… not bad in the circumstances.

As we taxied my gorgeous son vomited thoroughly over us both.

Hasty mopping was followed by a long queue at passport control.

'Madam, your son is in the wrong queue.'

Familiar words – but no less frustrating for that.

'Well, I could go and sit him down in the 'non-UK citizens' line to make his own way, then return myself to this one.'

'That won't be necessary… but get it sorted. He *must* have his own Australian passport'.

Patience frayed, energy dissipated and sense of humour in peril, I was inclined to ask how that would help the queuing situation. Instead, I smiled, promised that I would do so, and went through with as much dignity as our wet and smelly clothes would allow.

We have returned!

A British–Norwegian, **Elizabeth Pimm** was educated in the Nilgiri Hills of India, Oslo, Dublin, Perth and London. She worked in radio astronomy and vision research before running her own optometry practice in Cambridge. Since retirement she has restored an Italian farmhouse, invented a patented baby product and travelled widely. She is preparing to walk the Camino de Santiago. She has two enterprising children and three brilliant grandchildren.

Using Basketball Skills in a Chinese Hospital

Lori Green LeRoy

Some years ago, we were in Fuzhou, a small-by-Chinese-standards city of seven million people on the Taiwan Strait in Fujian province. Our hands were full. My husband Nick and I were there to adopt our son, Alex, who was just shy of three years old. The night we received custody and brought Alex back to our hotel room, I noticed that he was suffering from a low-level fever. I attributed this to stress and to the fact that he was wearing four layers of clothes despite the evening being warm. After all, Alex was eating fine and was generally happy bar getting used to the two strange faces now caring for and loving him. Our subsequent days were busy with adoption paperwork, going to appointments, strolling Alex around a lovely lake and park close to our hotel, and visiting some Fujian sights, notably amazing banyan trees and temples.

Then Alex's fever spiked and he started throwing up. I gave him some acetaminophen (paracetamol). This temporarily reduced his temperature, only for it to shoot back up once the medicine wore off. Worse still, Alex was not keeping anything down. Most fortunately, there was a health clinic at our hotel, to which we hurried. With the help of our Chinese guide-cum-translator, Penny, we gleaned that the doctor considered that Alex had a 'cold' and that we should give him warm tea. Twelve hours later, there was no improvement, so we returned. The doctor couldn't (or wouldn't) dispense a prescription and still offered no credible diagnosis. Dissatisfied with the physician's recommendations and nonchalance, we headed to the nearest hospital.

The timing could hardly have been worse. This was a critical day in the adoption process. If we were to avoid the week-long hiatus of Chinese New Year, we needed to finalise paperwork and obtain Alex's passport. Moreover, that afternoon we had to fly to another Chinese city to secure Alex's US visa and complete additional forms.

Nick had previous with Chinese hospitals having worked in Shanghai years previously. He had witnessed people smoking in the stairwells; had shared an elevator with someone who was in the process of getting a blood transfusion; and noticed that cash handed over via a handshake procured quicker and better service. His view was that if one of us became really ill, we should fly to Tokyo or Hong Kong as soon as possible.

That said, we had a sick baby and no other viable options. We called a cab and headed for the nearest hospital.

My fears were realised when traffic came to a standstill a few blocks from the hospital. We realised that this was due to a mass of cars trying (unsuccessfully) to reach the hospital. So, we hopped out of the car and, with Alex hoisted on my hip, walked the rest of the way.

I don't think I ever fully understood the term 'sea of humanity' until I saw the droves of people trying to pass through the hospital front door. Shoulder-to-shoulder, hundreds if not thousands of people were crowding every inch of space – even jamming into doorways and hallways. Forget the first day of the sales. The scrum just to see a doctor or nurse was something else. Whoever shoved and jostled his or her way to the front of the line (and held his or her ground) was seen next. Being passive did you no favours; politeness might mean waiting for hours.

Moving through the maze of hallways, there was a fuzzy soundtrack of yelling and moaning merging with bells and alarms, and an acrid, sweaty smell permeating the air. People with sallow skin and lifeless eyes were lying on wheeled stretchers, their bodies swathed in blood-stained gauze. I sidestepped yet more forms sleeping on the floor or falling out of wheelchairs. Keeping my head down, I trudged along, Alex stuck to my hip and his face buried in my chest.

I found a 'quieter' hallway in which to wait with Alex while Penny and Nick registered. The combination of hubbub and poor health made for a very unhappy child. Meanwhile, I was on the verge of a panic attack, swallowing bile and gritting my teeth. I paced and swayed with Alex, seeking to calm us both down.

Then I looked up. We were standing outside a room that made me think of the mental-health patients' ward in the film *One Flew Over the Cuckoo's Nest*. Bags of fluid cascaded from hooked poles that dropped from the ceiling. Patients stared into space while receiving treatments. Unclear whether these were blood transfusions, chemotherapy or something else, I kept our distance.

About ten minutes later Nick and Penny grabbed us, announcing that we could proceed to the paediatric room then push our way through to see a doctor. Surely this was good news?

Or not. We entered to find the world's most heinous game of musical chairs underway. About twenty adults plus their sick children were crowded in and around a tiny room that was barely eight feet by ten. Wary of airborne infection, all participants (except us) wore surgical masks. Everyone's attention was focused on a single point: the doctor sitting at a desk with a computer and lone chair. She examined a child as everyone else hovered over her. Kids were whimpering and coughing, their parents growing impatient and hunkering down, poised to rush forward as soon as the chair was vacated.

At school I played basketball for seven years and now put those sporting skills to good use. Continuing to clasp Alex and avoiding inhaling God-knows-what germs, I elbowed and hip-checked my way through several 'defenders' to reach the physician. The medic's attention was directed towards an infant with gauze around her head. The baby was tiny and weak. It pained me to think that this was the only way for a child to be seen by a doctor, even with an apparently serious condition.

But I didn't – *couldn't* – let this sympathy distract me from my mission. Our flight left in five hours, and it would take ninety minutes even to reach the airport. We had to see the doctor quickly, then leave immediately. Noticing a father and child ready to pounce as the parent ahead of me started to rise from the chair, a combination of mother bear and competitive basketball player came over me. Deploying my nice, wide American child-bearing hips, I blocked them out, hooked my foot around the leg of the chair, pulled it toward me and – legs spread and elbows sharpened – sat down. Victory!

Although surprised, the doctor had clearly witnessed such a tactic previously. She started examining Alex, asking questions through Penny. After three minutes, she handed me a prescription for antibiotics, vitamin B6 and acetaminophen. We clutched this life-saver-on-paper and scarpered.

Prescription converted into medicine, we made it back to the hotel just in time to pack our bags and meet the police officer who had Alex's passport. This was still delay enough for Alex to throw up over himself... and me. I cleaned up Alex pretty well with baby wipes and dressed him in clean clothes. I was less fortunate. Vomit leaked down into my bra and under my boobs. I wiped it off as best as I could and changed clothes, but my chest still smelled like sour milk and bananas throughout the long drive to the airport and subsequent flight. Just as well that my gag reflex is pretty weak.

The antibiotics worked miracles. Alex's fever broke within two hours. My boobs remained puke-free. We returned home safely – thanks to my first and best basketball coach, my dad. Without him sharing some great moves on court, we might still be in that hospital.

Lori Green LeRoy is a public-relations professional who pens tips and tricks for travelling with kids, destinations reviews and more on her blog w mapsmemoriesandmotherhood.com. She also writes for w wesaidgotravel. com and w kidtripster.com. As lifelong wanderlusters, she and her husband Nick are currently indoctrinating their two young boys into the wonder and awe of exploring the world. So far they have notched up 11 countries and 28 US states.

Fall in Mexico

Astrid Vinje

One of the joys of travel – but also one of its downsides – is that we often have no way of predicting what might happen. Despite taking all necessary precautions, nightmares can become reality. You just have to deal with any problems that occur as best you can.

My husband Clint and I were in a bed on the veranda of our friend Lieve's holiday house, overlooking the Pacific Ocean in southern Mexico. The night was pitch-black, and I fell asleep to the sound of waves crashing on to the cliffs below.

Our two children – eight-year-old Mira and five-year-old Julian – were sleeping in a nearby room, tucked into beds guarded by mosquito nets. The humidity lay heavily, prompting both kids to sleep without nightshirts. All was quiet. All was well.

Then a crash jolted me awake. It was very loud, like a bowling ball falling off a table. Then Mira shrieked with pain. In the darkness and groggy with sleep, she had failed to see a set of stairs and tumbled down, hitting her head against metal-lined steps.

I sprang out of bed and rushed towards my daughter.

At the foot of the stairs, Mira crouched, crying in pain. Bright red streaks ran along her back and blood was splattered on the floor. The sight shocked me. But instinct propelled me onwards and downwards.

Reaching Mira, I found her back to be covered with scrapes and bruises underneath the blood. Clint, Lieve and I cleaned Mira up and comforted her.

'It's going to be OK,' I assured Mira. '*You're* going to be OK.' I kissed her forehead.

'I feel like I'm going to throw up,' Mira replied, amidst the tears. 'My head hurts.' Alarm bells rang. I checked her hair. On the top of Mira's head was an inch-and-a-half-long gash, incised deep into her scalp. Blood was matting her thick black hair. 'OK,' I said, taking a deep breath and trying to remain calm. 'OK, it's going to be OK.'

But my heart started to pound faster. This was serious. This wasn't an injury that we could fix with a bandage and some kisses. We needed to get to a hospital. We needed professional medical attention.

I checked my watch. It was almost two in the morning. I wondered if anything would be open at this hour.

This was our first night in the small beach village of Puerto Angel. Earlier that day, we had arrived at nearby Puerto Escondido airport after spending two months living in the central Mexican towns of San Miguel de Allende and Guanajuato. While we loved this urban jaunt, we were itching to head to the beach and soak up some sun.

A sweet Belgian family we had met while in San Miguel de Allende offered to host us for the night in Puerto Angel. Lieve's husband Willem and their youngest daughter picked us up from the airport. After an hour winding through beach towns, we arrived at the family's spacious holiday house.

Paradise, I thought, as I entered.

The décor was rustic, but the view was amazing. From the outdoor seating area on the first floor and the veranda on the second floor, you could see the ocean glowing blue in the late-afternoon sun. In the distance, small tourist boats raced past. Paradise, indeed.

Willem and Lieve proved great hosts, treating us to a delicious spread of freshly caught tuna, grilled vegetables and free-flowing wine. Their three kids instantly got along with our pair. We made plans to do a sea safari the following day. After an evening of talking and playing, we settled in our respective beds to rest up for the marine adventure.

But at two in the morning, standing in the kitchen with Mira, trying to keep her calm, a sea safari was the last thing on my mind. Willem was frantically checking his phone to find a nearby hospital. I scrambled around the house, gathering clothes and shoes for Mira. Clint was waking Julian so that we could take him with us. Mira slumped in the kitchen, still wailing in pain.

The nearest hospital that was open at that time of night was half an hour's drive away. We piled into Willem's car and sped off. I held Mira's hand, trying to keep her from falling asleep or, worse, falling unconscious.

At the hospital, our rudimentary Spanish sufficed for the nurse to garner an idea of what had happened. Following discussion with a doctor, the nurse determined that stitches were needed.

Mira started to cry. Her body was shaking. 'I don't want to die,' she whispered. I held her tight and kissed her on the cheeks, wiping tears from her face. 'You're not going to die,' I reassured her. 'These doctors know what they're doing. You're going to be just fine.'

With each insertion of the needle, Mira screamed in pain. I held her hand tightly and soothed as best I could. 'I love you, Mira. You're so brave.' I had never felt more helpless as a mother than I did at that moment.

All I wanted to do was rewind time by a few hours. What could I have done to prevent this? Why didn't I leave a light on so Mira could see the stairs? Why couldn't both kids have slept closer to us? Julian had his head buried into Clint's chest, closing his eyes each time Mira cried. He was suffering in his own way too.

After the final stitch was in, the doctor levied instructions for keeping the stitches clean. 'Stay out of the sun,' he told us. 'Don't go swimming. Wash the area with soap and water.'

'I will prescribe antibiotics and pain killers,' he continued. 'Come back in a week to get the stitches removed.' We left the hospital and returned to Willem and Lieve's house, relieved that the incident hadn't been worse. On balance, we had got away lightly.

The next day, Mira was in good spirits. Although her back was still hurting from the fall, her head was not. Our plans for a sea safari were discarded. Instead, we spent the day playing cards. Come evening, the previous night's events seemed like a distant memory.

Before coming to Mexico, I did all I could to mentally prepare for anything that might possibly go wrong. We might have a car accident. Our kids might get attacked by animals. One might get terribly sick. Yet none of these fears deterred us from travelling. The benefits of offering our kids a life-changing experience unequivocally outweighed the potential problems.

Travelling to Mexico introduced our family to a culture rich in tradition and history. We took opportunities to learn traditional Mexican recipes, climb pyramids and even see migrating monarch butterflies. As a family, we grew closer and stronger during our trip.

In travel, as in life, we always take chances. As parents, we are permanently conducting risk assessments. We prepare for the worst and hope for the best. And when something terrible does occur, we respond as calmly and effectively as we can. What happened to Mira could have happened anywhere – back home as much as on the road. With hindsight, granted, I could have taken more precautions to prevent such an accident. I've learned to leave lights on in unfamiliar houses, for a start...

Astrid Vinje is a freelance writer with a fascination for discovering people's unique stories. An avid traveller with at least 30 countries under her belt, she loves experiencing new cultures with her husband and two kids. Originally from the Pacific Northwest of the  United States, Astrid and her family are currently travelling full time around the world. She writes about her travels on her family-travel website w thewanderingdaughter.com.

A Wild Bus Journey
Across Borneo

Sophie Beesley

The bus emergency-exit door swung open violently as we sped around a tight corner. I swiftly grabbed the handle and held it closed with one hand while clinging tightly to my sleeping two-year-old with the other. The scrap of shoelace tied to the handle was as effective at keeping the door closed as the driver's wet underpants dangling on the curtain rail above my head was at keeping the sun out of my eyes. 'Just a few more hours to go,' I silently hoped.

It was our usual spontaneous decision to take this trip. Within two weeks we'd booked flights and a hotel for our first night, and we were suddenly in sweaty, exotic Borneo.

Since having children, my husband and I had reluctantly decided we should slow down our travel a little. We thought it would be sensible to plan our journey better, take our time, not move around so much, and perhaps go to more 'normal' places. On our first family trip to Asia we tried (well, half-tried) to be a little more responsible, but our usual travel habits returned rather quickly so such 'sensible' ideas were abandoned. Once we got ourselves back off the beaten path, we learnt that not only did adventurous travel suit us better but it suited the children too.

The realisation that we all loved the excitement of exploration, hopping from place to place, the random destinations, meeting local people, eating local food, taking local transport, and the opportunities and challenges that came from travelling this way, came as a relief and a delight. From then on, we planned little and experienced lots, revelling in the joy of the unexpected.

We'd been in Borneo for no more than a few days when we were itching to be on the move again. Having explored Kinabalu National Park we were keen to get from there, on one side of Sabah, across to the Kinabatangan River on the other. As a wildlife conservationist, I was dreaming of revisiting a place I'd travelled to twenty years before so we could all see hornbills and the famous red apes (orang utans).

Exploring Borneo all those years ago had awakened a deep love of the planet and its diverse habitats and wildlife. This was the place that had influenced me to change career to study conservation and had prompted further travel, far and wide. Moreover, the boys (aged two and four) wanted desperately to see crocodiles. We knew we'd probably have to pre-book such a remote river trip, but our intrepid spirit didn't dampen, and we quickly searched online for somewhere responsible and locally run to guide us. The night before we were due to travel across Sabah, we called a promising-sounding local co-operative project called KOPEL, set on an oxbow lake in the rainforest right next to the Kinabatangan. We asked if they could have us and, thankfully, there was room aplenty. Easy!

The sun rose, and we swiftly gathered our things, ready to leave. We had been given some basic instructions that the bus would pass by, right outside our guesthouse, and that it would stop if we flagged it down. There would be one bus in the morning and a second bus later in the afternoon. After a quick breakfast we set our bags down next to the road and waited. The boys were excited to soon be on the move again (bus journeys are their definition of fun) and they sat eagerly. Despite being hot and dusty, with little shade and nothing much to do, the kids were tolerant – incredibly tolerant, in fact. Thankfully, today they were masters of keeping themselves amused with nothing more than a few stones and sticks while watching passing vehicles and people. We chatted, waited, fidgeted, waited and wondered when our bus might arrive.

Often, we flagged down approaching buses, only to find they weren't ours; our hearts rose and sank every time. Hopes of an early arrival soon turned to the realisation that we'd somehow missed the morning bus, so our fate was now resting on the last bus of the day which would arrive in a couple more hours, maybe. We chanced dashing back across the road to ask our guesthouse to make us a take-away lunch and sat back in the dust eating and waiting. Concerned onlookers kindly asked where we were going but looked blank when questioned about the reliability of the buses. We played a few card games and felt thankful that our children weren't yet old enough to need the stimulus of electronic gadgets. We waited seven long hours.

Suddenly there was a bus… and unexpectedly it was ours! We hurriedly chucked on the bags and the kids, then hopped on. The bus was almost full with locals and we were inevitably left with the rear seats. All travellers know that the seats at the back are the boneshakers that nobody wants. Well, these were *worse*. These particular back seats had unfortunately easy access to the toilets which smelt indescribably awful, making us retch every time the door opened. There was also a shower – well, rain dripping down on us from the broken skylight in the roof.

Then there was the emergency exit. An 'escape route' that was partially blocked by an additional seat bolted in front of it; my seat.

The emergency exit that was 'closed' with a shoelace in a futile attempt to prevent the door being an accidental departure point for those who dared to sit too close. The exhausted kids fell asleep instantly. So there I sat, in my uncomfortable predicament, holding both door and child, waiting for it all to be over.

The bus made more stops than expected and took longer than we had been led to believe, so when darkness fell and we stopped for a refuel (the bus and us), we had lost all hope of getting to our jungle camp that night. We called our hosts at KOPEL, who graciously offered to prepare beds for us in the local village so we could rest and travel to the camp the next morning instead. All expectations gone hours before, we resigned ourselves to writing off the day (and a day is a big loss when you are only away for two weeks). The children took the news in their stride; I felt so proud of these resilient, adventurous, mature yet still very little children that we had raised.

We had given the driver our destination and detected the usual confusion because we didn't want to get off the bus at the usual junction for foreigners following the tourist trail. Wanting to be dropped on the bank of a river, at night, in darkness, with two small children, was met with understandable doubt. So we called our hosts and asked them to reassure our concerned driver; the care people show when you travel with children is such a wonderful comfort.

Having waited and travelled all day, we finally arrived. Headtorches on, we stepped into the darkness and moments later were met by our host. Exhausted and expecting to be shown to our makeshift beds, we were a little bemused to be told that we were, in fact, going to still make it to our final destination that night. All tiredness pushed aside, we eagerly donned life jackets and boarded a longboat to head down the river into the jungle. The boys' bravery shone through as bright as the moon above us and their excitement at seeing torchlit crocodiles, sleeping monkeys, owls on the hunt and – upon eventual arrival at our simple jungle camp – a civet snooping around just metres from us, made for an unforgettable memory and one that has convinced us to continue travelling in this 'real' way again and again.

It's true to say that such travel with children does sometimes test you. In these sorts of situations, challenges can bring out the worst in you. You worry, 'what if this doesn't go as planned?', and frustrations build up. Then there are times when you bicker, and when the children drive you crazy, and when you stress about getting to places on time, and when you let yourself think everything would have been easier if 'we'd just bothered sorting something out in advance for once!'

But not this time. Sitting by the dusty road, surrounded by real life, travelling in this unhurried way; it felt free and carefree. In these moments, when we simply have to go with the flow, when we adapt to a country's pace and its easy-going attitudes, we 'put ourselves in the hands of the gods', as they say. That is when we feel like we are really travelling, really experiencing something that would never happen on a package holiday or even a trip organised in a little more than two weeks before leaving. This was all part of our adventure; the stuff that makes us feel a part of the world different to our own. Besides, it was nothing like as bad as the eighteen-hour wait for a barely working truck to cross the treacherous Route 5a in Madagascar on our honeymoon, or the time I landed in Quito in Ecuador but took a wrong bus and ended up a day further away from my work placement in the cloud forest. (I wonder why my strongest memories are always public transport related?)

We had the most perfect few days on the Kinabatangan. A family practically alone, together in the jungle, exploring the river with our wonderful guide Ali. We trekked, spotted wildlife and even planted trees, reforesting the rainforest which the boys made a vow to return to see in ten years' time. I am moved to think of that connection – their own trees and their own special memories – in a place somewhere across the world in a country already so dear to me. Let's just hope that in a decade they'll have fixed that emergency exit.

Sophie Beesley is a wildlife conservationist, educator and mum of two little adventurers-in-training. Sophie's work and travels have enabled her to work with extraordinary animals and remarkable people in wildlife research, nature-based youth projects and practical habitat conservation. To see more of Sophie's family travels and outdoor adventures, follow 📷 @lifewildadventures.

Kidding Around

WATERWORLDS

Adjusting to Life at Sea

Caspar and Nichola Craven

Caspar's view

It's 6.34 a.m. The light is just starting to come up. The sea lollops us around, waves bubbling along the hull of the *Aretha* on our first ocean crossing. The sounds of sleep are all around me. The dawning light signals the start of truly embracing our Atlantic Adventure.

Scheduled departure day was 23 November, but high winds and squalls delayed our start. The breeze in the marina touched 43 knots. We found and completed new jobs on the boat: repair work on the dinghy that hangs from davits on the stern of our boat *Aretha*, cleaning below decks, and spending more time discussing alternative sail combinations. All good, valuable stuff.

You could feel the buzz of start day – we all just wanted to get going: final trip to the minimarket to buy bread, new fishing lures for Columbus (aged seven), topping up the freshwater tanks and downloading the latest weather updates. Race or rally starts are always an amazing sight: over two hundred boats in a small space, crews settling down, preparing sails. We slowly motored north to get away from the pack, finding quiet water. We had three thousand miles to go and wanted to stay out of trouble with other boats, so hung back. *Aretha* was one of the last boats to cross the starting line, but we soon hoisted full canvas, making satisfying progress through the fleet, passing by other boats one by one.

Columbus had been itching to get out a fishing line, so we set up one of his new lures – a pink marlin shaker. In just an hour we heard the ratchet scream into action. I grabbed the rod as line streamed out of the reel. In my haste I forgot I was fishing for big Atlantic fish, not bass off the South Devon coast. My efforts to slow down the reel with my thumb on the spool were rewarded with a burnt finger. With a snap the line had gone, and we were fish less. Lessons learned for sure as I put burn gel on my thumb.

There is a classic saying to describe the navigation and routing across the Atlantic. You head south until the butter melts, then turn right and head west until you hit land. Heading south is about getting into the trade winds and warmer weather. The route across the Atlantic is pretty straightforward and in November to December the probability of good settled conditions is high.

Life aboard settled into a routine: the children waking and going to bed at the agreed times, meals and routine maintenance becoming established. Sleep patterns were adjusting to watches: sleep when your head hits the pillow during your three hours off at night and wake rapidly when called for the next watch. We humans readily adapt to different patterns – it just takes a little time.

There were still boats all around us the first night. On Day 2 it thinned out. Then there was a clear feeling of being in the middle of the Atlantic. The children were starting to get used to the idea of what lay ahead.

Bluebell (aged nine): 'Are we nearly there yet?'

Me: 'No.'

Bluebell: 'How far is it to go?'

Me: 'Several thousand miles.'

Bluebell: 'Oh.'

One of the greatest joys we found was the simplicity of sitting down and eating together, a practice so often forgotten in the bustle of daily life. Being 'off grid' and away from the always-live connection to the internet meant that phones and iPads got put away and the focus shifted to talking and being present with each other rather than immersed in a device.

The clocks shifted by one hour so we had 'happy hour' on deck basking in the sunshine, celebrating with music and a treasure hunt for the children. (Each time we changed the clocks upon passing between time zones, we marked the occasion with a 'happy hour' party.) The sea temperature was 28.2°C and it would only get warmer. This was what we'd been looking forward to.

For the first time on this trip Nichola had found her sea legs and recovered from sea sickness so joined me on my night watches. It was lovely to have the company and to see her on top form.

We also caught and lost our second fish. Next lesson learned: slow the boat down properly before bringing the fish in. Schoolboy error. Again.

* * *

Aretha was warming up down below – at night we wore only shorts and a T-shirt. We were firmly in the trade winds now, gliding along effortlessly at 8 knots. Life settled into a pleasant routine. We enjoyed light winds, occasional squalls, and moderate winds up to 20 knots or so. We saw few other boats and became a happy crew content in our own world. By now we were getting to know *Aretha*, testing different sail combinations and becoming much more familiar with the onboard systems and equipment. We were happy as a team, and the children settled. Kids love routines and we could easily have carried on for much longer. This was the sort of thing we had envisaged during our five years of planning.

When the wind becomes light and variable with sailing progress slow, what do you do? The answer is obvious: turn the cockpit into a swimming pool by closing off the cockpit drain seacocks and filling the space with buckets of seawater. The water temperature was 31.6°C. Result – three happy children splashing and playing in the cockpit, throwing buckets of water over each other. The simple things in life.

On another day we created International Adopt-a-star Day – a school project. 'Find a constellation or star, learn about it, draw a picture, and tell the rest of the crew about it.'

Here are the stars or constellations we chose:

Bluebell: Draco the Dragon.

Columbus: Dorado.

Nichola: Perseus.

Willow (aged two): Cassiopeia (because it looks like a 'W').

Caspar: the Northern Cross (also called Cygnus the Swan).

I'm sure a psychologist could have a field day working out what those choices mean.

* * *

Every day on *Aretha* we instigated a tradition of 'values prizes'. We gave them during breakfast every day, singling each and every person for a specific behaviour or action that they had taken that was in accordance with our values of 'Laugh, Love, Action, Go Prepared, Understanding, Happy and Learn Something'. Each child had a wall chart and they'd get a sticker to place in the column for the value they had demonstrated that day – for example, Understanding. By consistently talking about the positive behaviours and what we appreciated, we were ingraining an attitude of focusing on what was right rather than what was wrong. Over time, we would get the children to run the values awards discussion so that they became versed in looking for good behaviours and praising other people for specific things they had done, no matter how big or small.

* * *

Nichola's view

Just finished morning school with the children. They don't seem to mind that it's Saturday – sticking to the conventional Monday to Friday school week doesn't work. Today we covered geography, oceans and sea, which is a Year Five topic for geography and fits perfectly with where we are at the moment. We are participating in a conservation project studying microplastics in the Atlantic. By asking a hundred boats to each collect six bottles of water as we crossed the Atlantic, the goal is to collect six hundred bottles of water mid-ocean, and then discerning the level of microplastics present. The findings will be published in *National Geographic*. Combining the research project with schooling brought the topic more to life.

After the success of the cockpit paddling pool yesterday, the plan today is to repeat the fun, though Caspar has suggested we put Fairy Liquid in the water and hand out sponges so that the children can clean the decks at the same time. I don't believe he's joking!

We are going to make fruit-juice ice lollies today as our freezer is now working perfectly. Bluebell is cooking lunch – pizza. She made one the other day and it was quite tasty. She could do with learning about cleaning while cooking: I kept finding brownie mix everywhere for at least another day after she baked those treats.

Today is Improvisation Day. We have all given each other a regular object – for example a pencil – and by the end of the day we each have to work out a new use for that object. Columbus gave me my object – duct tape!

Willow is sleeping at the moment – which is why I have the time to sit and write this email. She really is like a Duracell bunny. As soon as she awakes she operates at 100 percent. It's December, so the children have been opening their advent calendars each day, but Willow has already ploughed through fifteen of her days. Initially I was stopping her but then decided it will be easier once the chocolates inside have gone – so I am leaving her to it. She is picking up how Caspar gives out the skipper values awards each day. Today she got her books and started handing them out as prizes. Although sweet, she needs to spend some time on her delivery; as she handed them out to everyone she said: 'Do you want one?'

We have roast beef today to mark crossing the 2,000 nautical miles mark. We have 904.3 nautical miles left to go. It's getting hot now, so I am sitting here writing in a bikini and shorts. The children certainly have the advantage that they can walk around in their underwear. I am not too unhappy with that as it saves on laundry!

* * *

Some highlights from a typical day crossing an ocean
1. Watching a pod of dolphins play alongside *Aretha*.
2. Discovering a flying fish on deck – after someone stood on it!

3. Catching a dorado at first light – filleted and sliced for sashimi followed by curry.
4. Bluebell playing guitar to the crew during our evening meal – a piece she'd written herself.
5. Columbus baking his first loaf of bread – the young man justifiably proud of his efforts.
6. Running the water maker – it's immensely satisfying to make fresh drinking water from seawater.
7. Enjoying hot showers – managing water and power means hot showers only every five days.
8. Checking rigging, sails and generator.

Adapted from *Where the Magic Happens: How a Young Family Changed their Lives and Sailed Around the World* (© Caspar Craven, 2018; Adlard Coles Nautical, an imprint of Bloomsbury Publishing Plc). Reproduced with the publisher's kind permission.

Caspar and Nichola Craven are co-founders of personal development company The Brave You. Caspar is the author of *Where the Magic Happens* (details as above) which  details the family's sailing voyage around the world, a trip that defined their life and business philosophy.

The Voyage to Wild Cat Island

Amy-Jane Beer

O ur son Lochy was born in 2011, not long after we'd bought an old house. The perfect storm of a semi-detached money pit, unpaid maternity 'leave' and economic austerity put horrible pressure on the combined incomes of a teacher and a freelance writer. For several years since, family travel has been mostly confined to places we can reach in a car laden with camping equipment. We know the wide world is still out there, but, because we've become such avid explorers of our own land, there's been no real sense of missing out.

Discovering or rediscovering parts of the UK and seeing its variety through the unprejudiced eyes of a child has been an unexpected gift. Having slept under outback stars, heli-kayaked white-water canyons, bounced on to the runway of the highest commercial airport in the world, seen glaciers and boiling mud and explored barrier reefs, mountains, rainforests and deserts, it is easy to forget that, as children, we could have made an adventure from a cardboard box, a bale of straw, a single small tree or a puddle. By that that measure, Britain is a limitless wonderland.

Lochy believes he has explored. He's climbed mountains of his own, canoed rivers and lakes, wild camped and stargazed, biked and hiked, surfed and swum. He's keen on wildlife and has seen plenty, even in his home county – starling murmurations, one of the world's largest colonies of gannets, and minke whales. Last month he watched a wild stoat killing a wild rabbit from a distance of no more than three metres – a spectacle whose intensity and immediacy might not be matched in a year of safari. But ask him for the place that he most remembers, the adventures he has loved best, and there's a common theme. It's the islands.

Perhaps that's not surprising. Islands of one sort or another have a special allure for most of us, I suspect, be they remote sun-drenched paradises or slimy platforms with a duck house in a municipal boating lake.

And this is especially true when you're small. In Lochy's view, the smaller and less inhabited the island the better, and the best of all islands is the first he remembers visiting. It's also one of the tiniest, though it could hardly command a bigger place in his imagination. Most maps of the Lake District call it Peel Island – but fans of Arthur Ransome's blissful *Swallows and Amazons* adventure series will know it as Wild Cat Island. They will also know that properly, you should have no map, but make one for yourself. You should pack your rations and a few other useful items – telescope, pocket knife, Jolly Roger flag – and set forth onto uncharted waters. Your craft may look like a canoe, a sit-on-top-kayak, an inflatable dinghy or (if you're really going for authenticity) a sailing boat rented in Coniston, but you know that really, it is a pirate brig or a raft you have cobbled together from bits of shipwreck.

On reaching the small island huddled close to the southeastern shore of the lake, you find your way in among the rocks to the hidden harbour. You disembark, watchful for natives, and you explore every track, every cluster of trees, every cliff and lookout, every rocky corner, and then you plant your flag and declare the island yours forever.

This, in essence, was the plan on a cloudless May morning when we shoved off from a stony beach on the western shore. We'd brought our own canoe, which accommodates three, but had spiced up the challenge by wrestling a six-month-old Border collie into a life jacket and coaxing her aboard. It was beguilingly warm, the lake and the fells blazed in saturated Instagram hues.

Ten minutes later we launched again after stopping for the wee Lochy remembered he needed moments after we set off the first time. A further ten minutes after that we realised he was missing the sun hat he'd set out in. On questioning, he thought he might have left it by the weeing tree. In the interests of making progress, we decided to press on and try to retrieve it on our way back: 'Here, you can wear Daddy's hat for now'. Roy proffered the cap he usually wears for running. It's nothing special, but Lochy was pleased with it.

Some time later, just as we attempted to push out from the shore towards the island on the other side, the breeze picked up. Funnelled by the fells, it blew almost straight down the lake, driving the well-laden boat sideways, away from the island and back towards the western shore. Our progress suddenly required constant correction, and the comfortable lapping of water under the bow was replaced by abrupt slapping on the port side.

In the space of two minutes, our lazy stokes became laboured, and in the space of five we realised we'd made a mistake in not crossing sooner. From where we were, we couldn't continue to alter our approach without turning fully sideways to the wind – and already it was strong enough that doing so would be difficult and unstable.

We decided to carry on into the shelter of the next bay, then attempt to cross the lake at the narrowest point. 'We'll have to do it by heading into the wind,' Roy shouted from the stern. 'It'll be harder work, but we'll be able to keep on course, and if we pick the right place it won't be long before we gain the shelter of the eastern shore.'

He wasn't kidding about hard work. There was no flow on the lake but the wind forced us to paddle as though we were crossing a river – angling the boat well upstream of our destination and pushing hard against the current, seeking to compensate for the ground we would lose.

By halfway, my shoulder muscles were starting to flood with lactic acid, and the boy was starting to fret. Partly it was that the wind was chilly, and our paddles were spattering him with water, but he'd also picked up the vibe. It's nigh on impossible to keep up cheery chatter when you're paddling as hard as you can. Lochy fidgeted, was told sharply to sit still, and suddenly he didn't like it any more.

You read things from time to time about canoes with children in, capsizing in the middle of chilly lakes. And we often see boats heading out in which nobody is wearing dry kit or a buoyancy aid – or perhaps only the children are. It gives me the absolute willies. British lakes are cold, most of the year, especially the deep ones. And if you're not used to it, cold affects your ability to swim, to think, or do anything useful. If the adult is in trouble, the kids are too.

We were kitted up. Personal flotation devices all round, dog included, and buoyancy bags in the boat. None of us would sink, no matter what. But still, I've not had to work so hard with Lochy in the boat before and I was stressed. A sudden strong gust of wind elicited a long wail… 'Daddy's haaaat!' It had blown off Lochy's head and into the water. The boat lurched and lost momentum as Roy made a single unsuccessful attempt to catch it with his paddle. One lost stroke was lesson enough. 'Forget it, keep going.'

'But... Daddy's hat!'

There was no way I was going to turn our boat broadside to this wind in the very middle of the lake. We tried to explain, in short, breathless sentences, that we couldn't stop, or turn, or go back, and that Daddy had other hats. But in the moment of loss, this inanimate, easily replaceable object had gained disproportionate sentimental value, and Lochy was beside himself. He could see the hat still, bobbing inexorably ever-further behind us, and our wilful betrayal was beyond his comprehension. He started to howl, like Tom Hanks's character Chuck Noland sobbing for Wilson the volleyball in the film *Cast Away*.

A deep burn in the deltoid muscles and a heart thudding with exertion makes it hard to find soothing words or tone. So for a couple of minutes we just dug in, letting him cry and protest. And then, suddenly, we'd done it, and it was like gaining the crest of a hill on a pushbike. The resistance wasn't gone, but the boat was suddenly gliding rather than lurching. A few more strokes and it was safe to make a turn, then cruise downwind towards the island. My arms felt like spaghetti. Lochy was still crying.

But then we were sliding past a low tree-lined cliff that tapered to a rocky promontory. As we rounded the end and nosed the boat into the lee of the rocks, we found ourselves in perfect shelter. The sun was delicious, the water clear and quiet – and Lochy realised where we were. 'It's the hidden harbour!' And so it was, exactly as he knew it from the books, a tiny landing place, guarded by phalanges of smooth, grey, sun-warmed rocks, and trees clustering like curious onlookers.

He was first ashore, splashing a bit, holding the painter as we unloaded, and positively vibrating with anticipation. And the island didn't disappoint. We stayed a couple of hours, in which he explored every square metre, from hidden harbour to camping place, to lookout point. Lochy beat the bounds of his new territory, checking the entire waterline, just in case, against all odds, the cap had washed up. It hadn't, but when Roy sat down to eat lunch, he wriggled uncomfortably for a moment, then patted his bum, and with puzzled frown giving way to rueful grin, pulled the original sun hat from the rear pocket of his shorts.

Amy-Jane Beer is a biologist and nature writer. She earned a doctorate studying sea urchins before swapping the microscope for a keyboard. She is the author of several non-fiction books on science and natural history, writes regularly for *The Guardian*, *BBC Wildlife* and *Countryfile*, is a columnist for *British Wildlife* and is working on her first, nature-inspired novel. She lives in North Yorkshire with her husband, nature- and Lego-obsessed son, and turbo-charged Border collie.

River Journey

Jonathan Lorie

'Do you think Coke is good for me, out here?' Her cheeks are flushed with the midday heat and her Tintin T-shirt is wet with fear. Around us hippos thrash in the water and a crocodile stares from the shore. I lean into the bows and fish an ice-cold can from a wooden box. 'I'm sure it is,' I smile and she takes a long slow sip. 'Do you think,' she whispers, 'chocolate is good for me, out here?'

This morning at dawn when we boarded the narrow canoe, accompanied by a ranger with a rifle, she did seem a little nervous. Our guide took one look and sat right beside her. 'Do you know,' he murmured, 'the story of the leopard and the warthog?' And by the time he'd finished his ancient tale we were way downstream, where egrets waded through tall rushes and clouds of pink birds flittered in our wake.

Slowly the river woke to the day. 'Elephants at nine o'clock!' yelled the ranger above our chugging engine, as giants emerged from acacia trees and shambled to the water for a drink. Zebras skittered through rippling grasses and guinea fowl pecked in the yellow mud. Hippos under the water were the best, she shouted, because you could spot them by their bubbles. 'Maybe,' she laughed, 'Moomintroll is a hippo?'

Six months ago she said to me, walking home from primary school, 'Daddy, take me to Africa.' That day her homework was to write about a hero and the one she chose was Joy Adamson, the lion-protector from Kenya. It was my fault, I suppose, after filling her head with adventures and misadventures of my own in various parts of the continent. So I paid my dues and bought the flights. And here we were, four planes in, floating down a flooded river somewhere in southern Zambia.

Every one of those flights had been a purgatory for her, unused as she was to aircraft. On the very first, two hours out from London, I realised too late that the box of sickness pills I had carefully packed was actually empty: and on each of those planes my lovely daughter was sick as a dog. She missed the classic views unrolling beneath us of green forests sliced by the brown loops of lazy rivers. She missed too the rising spray of Victoria Falls, 'the smoke that thunders', whose curtain of mist I saw from thirty miles away. But she never flinched. She boarded every plane, even the twelve-seat Cessna that trembled its way through the clouds, knowing what lay in store for her.

'Brave as a lion,' I whispered in her ear each time as I handed her the sick bag. And then we landed, finally, bumping to a stop on a strip of grass near the South Luangwa National Park. Africa smelt of charcoal and earth. We flopped into a jeep and as forest gave way to plots of maize between mud-walled huts, she started to smile. Women in bright scarves waved. She pulled the bobble from her long blond hair and it flickered in the breeze as we rattled along. 'It's so calm here,' she sighed, 'all the people are friendly. I'd like all my friends to see this.'

Luangwa is David Livingstone's backyard, and he crossed this river just fifty miles from here, back in the 1860s. It still felt fairly remote. When we rolled into a safari lodge, with its thatched houses and clipped lawns, I thought this was how his mission stations must have been, lost and found deep in the bush.

'Would you like to see a hippo?' asked the lodge's owner, Christina Carr, and walked my daughter to the edge of a pool that was filled with lilies and edged by giant termite hills. 'I came here one summer to work,' I heard, 'sixteen years ago, and somehow I never left. Perhaps you'll be the same.'

And that night we sat by the pool on a teak veranda lit by paraffin lamps as bullfrogs croaked in the water and the great African moon lit a vista of silvery grasslands where gazelles wandered and lions coughed.

But next morning, when a green snake slithered between our chairs on the lawn, she turned to me and said, 'Daddy, this is hotel Africa. I want to see the real Africa.'

So we boarded a canoe and sailed upriver. Just like in a story.

The Luangwa River in the rainy season is empty of people and full of life. She loved it, until the crocodiles. We saw them first asleep on the banks, twelve feet long, their jaws propped open as though ready to strike. Then they were in the water. We only knew where they were by the pairs of eyes gliding across the swirling current. They did not blink.

A hippo reared up, grunting madly, its massive body not comical now, its heavy fangs curving through the air. A crocodile must have startled it. A second gave chase and then the river was a boiling mass of growling creatures, startled from their siestas into noisy argument. The guide jerked the rudder and we swung out from trouble and then stopped, dead, stuck in midstream. 'We're on a mudbank!' he yelled. The hippos eyed us angrily.

The guide cut the engine and there was silence. Waves slapped the steel sides. The ranger fingered his rifle. We did not move.

The hippos looked away. Slowly they slipped under water, grumbling to each other. The crocs had gone. The river caught us and we drifted on, while the guide fussed the engine back to life. Then he revved it to a roar, filling the air with smoke and sending the wildlife racing for cover. He chuckled as we sped away.

'Chocolate,' I announce, 'is never exactly good for you, even out here. But it does make you happy. Which is pretty good anywhere.'

She seems pleased with this and relaxes as we turn into a narrow channel where baboons scamper in the branches overhead. Doves call and a fish eagle swoops low across our bows. The guide moors us to a mangrove tree and smiles, 'Shall we take a walk?'

We clamber onto the bank behind the ranger and creep among the trees, looking for moving shapes. The guide points ahead. He's seen a pair of huge grey ears, flapping among thorn trees, and slowly a herd of elephants wanders out of the shade. My daughter is enthralled. We sit and watch for longer than I knew she could, until they amble away. Then the guide explains an elephant's family structure.

He picks up a stick and prods a six-inch millipede as thick and black as a licorice stick. 'Do you know,' he asks her, 'how long it takes this one to put on his boots?' And he's off on another folk tale, his hands carving pictures in the air. Then he shows her a trail of Matabele ants: 'Hear them sizzle? They are angry.'

As we stroll back to the boat I thank him and he replies softly, 'It is alright. I am a father too.'

The sun sets over the water while we putter slowly to our camp for the night. It's a simple place on a sandy bank where we will sleep in huts of woven reeds. Creaking open the door to ours, we're buzzed by a big black insect with angry yellow wings and she bursts into tears. It's been rather a day.

I wave away the buzzer and show her inside. We have beds looking out on a creek and behind them there's a washroom with a tree growing out of the floor. I persuade her to take a cooling shower and step out to the deck in front. She shrieks. I run back. She's standing under the shower now, laughing fit to bust. A four-inch frog is hopping around the shower tray, croaking at her angrily. Just like in a story.

After dark we wander to the shore, where a firepit holds a heap of logs, flaming and crackling. Sparks rise into the velvet air like fireflies and merge with the burning stars overhead.

Stepping out of the darkness, our guide starts talking about the kinship bonds in his family group, the Elephant Clan, and how they help each other. They still have chiefs with local power, but women want independence. My daughter's eyes are wide. I ask what he's learnt in his 18 years of guiding among the wildlife. He pauses.

'The animals are not like us,' he muses. 'They are more peaceful. They may not look so, but they do not fight like us to be front of the queue. We are competitive. They take more time.' He giggles. 'And you in the West, you take even less time than we do here. You have watches, but we have time.'

The river whispers behind us and bushbabies whoop in the trees. I glance across at my daughter, who has come so far and learned so much since leaving London a week ago. She is staring into the fire.

Jonathan Lorie is a travel writer specialising in culture, history, wilderness and wildlife. He leads the Travellers' Tales training agency and his book *The Travel Writer's Way* (Bradt Travel Guides, 2019) is a complete guide for travel writers at all levels, whether for publication or just for fun.

Bali

Ginny Whitelaw

The grainy, flickering 1990s video was just showing feet rushing through sand. Bare feet, feet in flip-flops, tanned feet with white marks where sandals had been. The shouting was urgent, desperate, unintelligible. Sand became rock; rock became water and then, then – abruptly, rudely – there was nothing but flickering, blank footage.

I sat on the floor as the sun streamed through the cottage window. I switched off the old VHS player and I cast my mind back...

* * *

The flight from London Heathrow to Denpasar on the Indonesian island of Bali had been long and anything but straightforward, involving as it did a six-hour stopover in Hong Kong. At the outset, our four children were excited and positive at the adventure. In a short time, however, Toby kept kicking Arabella's seat when she allowed it to recline, saying in his loudest, most pompous voice (if an eight-year-old can sound pompous), 'It's so unfair! I've got nowhere to put my legs. Make her go forward, Mum!'

Aware that Toby was not going to stop yelling, I sought to distract him. 'There'll be a film on in a minute, Tobes. Shall we have a look and see what it is?'

'Only if SHE puts her seat forward,' he grumbled. So much for me being able to indulge myself by gazing mindlessly at clouds beyond the window.

Cue a small hand tugging at my sleeve. I turned to see four-year-old Mary beside me. I bent down. 'Darling, you shouldn't be out of your seat! There's a film on in a minute.'

'But Charlie's crying,' Mary said, pulling my hand and pointing across the aisle. I breathed in. Two-year-old Charlie was my husband David's responsibility. And David, although sitting beside Charlie, was fast asleep – seat reclined, eye mask on, mouth wide open.

'Wait for the film,' I advised an increasingly crotchety Toby as I crossed the aisle to unbuckle Charlie and cradle him in my arms, while simultaneously gently guiding Mary back to her seat beside David. 'Thanks, poppet,' I mouthed to Mary, as I felt my lap dampen with the reason for Charlie's distress, just as the plane began to dip and the seatbelt signs came on again.

I would love to have seen Hong Kong, but after the repeated turbulence and the inevitable argument with David, it was all we could do to negotiate the transit signs in the unfamiliar airport and drag the children along with us. That said, we did try dim sum in the transit lounge, but Toby's ensuing choking and retching did nothing to endear our family to our fellow passengers.

Back on the plane, with David suitably admonished and sitting firmly between Toby and Arabella, the short hop to Denpasar passed uneventfully. I had high hopes for Bali. White sand leading to a turquoise ocean. Two magical straw houses on stilts in a rainforest clearing – each with a veranda, slippers and chocolate on the pillows. 'The ladies bow at us,' marveled ten-year-old Arabella as I helped her unpack. 'Why do they fold their hands like that? Are they praying?' I think it's a gesture of greeting,' I replied. 'You might like to do it back to them.'

'Mum,' a freshly bathed and sleepy Toby murmured as I tucked him in, 'Dad said we can go jet-skiing tomorrow!'

Now was not the time to dissent. 'Yes, maybe,' I replied, making no commitment. 'We'll have to see how old you need to be.'

Trust David to make such a unilateral and unhelpful promise. I started to berate him. But as we sipped Singapore Slings on the veranda, the swooshing sea and rustling of leaves by manifold unseen insects – together with David smiling at me – calmed my nerves. I knew I would sleep well that night.

The following morning – the first of our holiday – will remain with me forever. All the children smiling and laughing at the vast buffet breakfast. Everything decorated with purple orchids and deep pink bougainvillea. The staff delighted to help us choose freshly made tropical juices, scrambled eggs and delicious *cha siu bao* (steamed buns with sweet pork in the middle). We walked the few yards to the beach and the harbour, where slight Indonesian ladies carrying trinkets called to us, 'You come in my sop?' And specifically to me: 'we have big size, lady!'

Mary led Charlie as he toddled on to the sand, his face a picture of pure joy. Toby spotted the jet skis straight away. He yanked at his father's shirt, begging to be allowed on one. 'It'll be ok,' David insisted, seeing the fear spread across my face. 'They explain everything to the children, I've seen them. Arabella is older, so she can go first.' I wasn't worried about my sophisticated, sensible Arabella – but Toby was something else entirely. He was never going to listen to instructions.

'Don't be a killjoy, love.' David was already following Toby towards a huge yellow machine and Arabella was clambering onto a scarlet one. A young boy, not much older than Arabella, was showing her the controls and she was nodding, setting off across the water, full-throttle, within seconds. The noise was deafening, but Arabella held her hand up in triumph and I noticed that her other arm was joined to the handlebar by a wristband.

David had his new video camera around his neck and began filming as he yelled, 'Go, Ari, go!'

'What about *me*?' sulked Toby. But before I could answer, I saw that David had started running – no, sprinting – towards the harbour wall. I watched, frozen, as Arabella sped over the water towards the very same wall – without the jet ski slowing even a fraction.

Dropping my bag, I hurtled after David (now shouting 'let go!') just as the machine thumped into the harbour wall and flew into the air. Arabella's screaming, limp body careered over the top of the barrier and fell out of sight behind it. For a split second, all I could hear was silence. And then everyone on the beach was running and, in my head, I was yelling 'What's behind the wall? Sand? Water? Rocks? Oh my God... What's behind the harbour wall?'

* * *

I stood up, my whole body shaking, the tears of a fractured almost thirty-year-old memory coursing down my crumpled face. It was at that moment that the telephone rang.

'Mum? Are you OK?' It was Arabella's excited voice. 'Mum, I wanted to run something past you. We're planning a holiday with the kids... in Bali. If I promise no jet skis, would you like to come?'

Ginny Whitelaw is a retired Cornish drama teacher, mother of four and grandmother of seven. She has worked as a radio broadcaster in Korea, theatre director in Hong Kong and teacher in both Switzerland and the UK. She travelled extensively with her children  in Asia. Ginny has studied Creative Writing and is an active participant in groups writing for children and adults.

CULTURAL
ENRICHMENT

Back to Our Roots

George Bernard Shaw

'Daddy,' said my seven-year-old daughter Belle, coming into the study to interrupt my work. 'Do you remember roots?'

'Roots of what?' I answered absent-mindedly. 'Farimang says that everybody in the world watched roots on TV,' she continued. 'Oh, you mean the programme *Roots*?' I replied, suddenly alert. It was a series I had watched as a teenager about an African boy who was captured and sold into slavery.

Having just completed my law studies, I had taken up a six-month internship at a human-rights charity based in Banjul, capital of The Gambia. Although it meant leaving Belle and my wife Alice behind in London, I knew that the stint would afford valuable career experience. I rented a small house in the beach resort of Kololi, just south of Banjul. This came with a 'houseboy' called Farimang Taal. He was no longer a boy, being in his forties, and he knew little about housekeeping – but he was both enthusiastic and desperately poor. When the house wasn't being rented out, he earned his living selling trinkets to visitors. When I arrived, the winter tourist season had come to an end, and Farimang needed money.

At Easter, Alice and Belle came to The Gambia for a three-week holiday. Although I had to work during the week, I thought they would be happy enjoying the beach, playing in the sand and splashing in the Atlantic waves not more than fifteen minutes' walk from the house. If and when that palled, there were always swimming pools at the luxury hotels to enjoy.

I needn't have worried. Belle swiftly developed a friendship with Farimang, following him as he went about his chores. They would water plants in the courtyard garden, sweep the house and go shopping for groceries. She even helped with the washing-up. Farimang's method of cleaning crockery involved pouring copious amounts of washing powder into the bowl and then – much to Alice's annoyance – rinsing the dishes in gallons of our precious water supply.

When it came time for Farimang, a devout Muslim, to say his regular prayers, Belle would watch transfixed as he laid out his prayer mat on the floor facing Mecca and then went through the various genuflections. She would peer round the door, clutching a precious cuddly toy. Afterwards we would find Belle in her bedroom, with Hush the basset hound, practicing moves copied from Farimang.

Over the next few days, Belle pestered Alice and I about 'Roots' until finally I asked Farimang what stories he had been telling her. 'No stories,' said Farimang. 'All true.'

It turned out that Farimang came from a village on the far side of the Gambia River, the great body of water that bisected the West African nation. He claimed that he was distantly related to Kunta Kinte, the 18th-century hero of Alex Haley's 1970s novel and subsequent TV series. Farimang had been telling Belle about the village of Juffureh where both he and Kunta Kinte were born, mixing up the realities of a remote African hamlet with the glitz and glamour of Hollywood. It was a long time since Farimang had been back to see his wife, baby son or family; it was obviously his intention to use Belle's influence to persuade us to visit Juffureh with him as our guide. Belle's persistence paid off and we agreed to make a day trip to Farimang's home on the last Saturday of the holiday.

Farimang was very excited and set about planning the trip, asking for an advance in wages in order to buy gifts for his family. Rising at dawn, we waited for him to turn up with a taxi. The morning was misty but the tropical sun was starting to break through the clouds. At 7 a.m., Farimang finally arrived in an old Mercedes car, one of the many taxis that cruised the few paved roads of The Gambia. He jumped out of the passenger seat and ran towards us.

'So sorry,' he gasped. 'The battery no spark. We push taxi long time and now we are late.' We piled into the car, me in the front passenger seat and Farimang in the back with Alice, Belle and Hush, who was stuffed into Belle's small rucksack with his head and floppy ears poking out of the top. The taxi sped away along dusty back streets to the port of Banjul.

When we reached the quayside, we were greeted by chaos. Cars and trucks lined up, waiting to board the ferry. People thronged around the entrance to the terminal, a shed that was already stiflingly hot as the morning sun beat down on its metal roof. The crowd pressed towards the gate that separated us from the ferry. Farimang held Belle tightly by the hand as the swell of bodies moved us along. Suddenly the metal gate, now just a few feet in front of us, clanged shut. A roar of frustration went up from the crowd. Farimang turned and looked at us in despair. 'I think we have literally missed the boat,' I said to Alice.

As the crowd subsided, each person sought out a corner of the stuffy shed in which to sit and wait for the next ferry. I asked Farimang when it would depart. 'Maybe in four hours?' he said. 'Well there's no way we can get to Juffureh and back in one day then,' said Alice pragmatically. 'We might as well go home now.'

But Farimang wasn't going to give up that easily. He had an idea. Scooping Belle up in his arms, he pushed his way out of the shed and made for the riverbank. We hurriedly followed.

The Gambia River stretched out before us, a huge expanse of calm water that flowed west towards the Atlantic Ocean. The far bank – some two miles away – was barely visible. Several enormous and brightly painted canoes, 150 feet long or more, were anchored at the water's edge. Farimang was talking to a man beside one of them. As we approached, we could see he was smiling. 'We will take canoe taxi,' he said, pointing at the boat in front of him.

Belle was excited at the prospect of travelling in this big boat. It certainly was a fine specimen, long and sleek with a painted prow that shot majestically upwards towards the blue sky. We waded through the shallow water and climbed aboard. There were no seats, just planks of wood laid crossways. More travellers had followed us down to the riverbank, carrying metal pans, baskets and bags of produce. They climbed on board. The canoe started to fill up. A donkey cart arrived laden with sacks of rice and flour. These were deposited beneath the prow. Alice sat with Belle, shaded from the sun under an umbrella, and trailed her fingers in the river. As the canoe became ever fuller, the boat sank lower and lower in the water. After an hour of waiting, and as more people and more cargo were loaded, we began to get concerned.

'When will it leave?' I asked Farimang.

'Soon, soon,' he said.

Now the top of the canoe was barely six inches above the water surface. Was this the most sensible thing to be doing with a seven-year-old child in tow? But Belle was enjoying herself and had made friends with some Gambian girls. With a sudden growl, the outboard motor kicked into life. The ropes that tied the canoe to the shore were thrown on board – and we were off. The cooling breeze coming off the river was refreshing after the heat of the riverbank. We sped across the river into an expanse of empty water. The crowd of passengers chattered and joked. One man spotted dolphins up ahead, and we admired the grey curves of their bodies cutting through the water on their way to the ocean.

Then disaster struck. The outboard motor suddenly died. Silence descended on the canoe. The helmsman and his mate pulled and poked the machine. They jerked the blade out of the water and examined it. Slowly, inextricably, we began to drift towards the sea. The ferry had long since departed. There were no other vessels in sight.

Alice looked grim, her jaw set. She was probably imagining the worst possible outcome – being swept out to sea and crushed by mighty Atlantic waves. In the bowels of the canoe a muttering and a murmuring started. Tiny prayer books were produced and beads fingered as a hundred Muslims prayed for salvation. For what seemed like an eternity, the canoe sat becalmed. Only the sound of waves slapping the vessel's side could be heard above the mumbled prayers. Then the outboard motor let out a screech. The blade was thrust back into the water and the canoe jolted forward again, away from the looming ocean. A great cry of *Hamdulillah* ('praise be to God') rose up amid audible sighs of relief.

As the canoe came to rest on the far bank, muscled youths stripped naked to the waist appeared, wading thigh-deep through the water to carry off passengers and cargo. They shouted up at Alice then carried her off the boat and onto dry land. Farimang and Belle followed, while it required two 'porters' to manhandle me to the shore. Farimang hailed a bush taxi, a beaten-up Peugeot estate the colour of the sandy earth. Then we were off again, bouncing over the rutted road and following the river inland towards its source. The track cut its way through scrubby bushes and gnarled, dried-up trees.

Eventually we reached Juffureh, a riverside hamlet. Despite its claim to fame, Juffureh was a dusty, impoverished place. Farimang proudly took us to his house, a mud-brick structure topped by a rusty corrugated-iron roof. At some point in the distant past, the walls had been painted blue but were now softly turning brown as they blended into the dry soil. The windows were mere holes shuttered against the burning sun by further corrugated iron. Farimang's wife and family were sitting on the makeshift terrace outside. Their jaws dropped amid astonishment and delight at our arrival to see us. Farimang's baby son was brought out to be passed around and admired.

Then Farimang took us off to meet the village VIP. A wizened old lady sat in state on a wooden bench inside an open-fronted shed. She was introduced as Binta Kinte, a seventh-generation descendant of Kunta Kinte's sister. We smiled and bowed and looked suitably impressed. Binta produced torn photographs and tattered yellowing newspaper cuttings of visiting dignitaries who had come to pay her court. We took photographs and gave her some money. She didn't smile once but Farimang was nevertheless over the moon. Not only had he been able to visit his family, but he'd brought influential visitors with him too. For him, the day had been a great success.

After a brief meal of rice and tomato sauce cooked by Farimang's wife, we jumped back into the taxi and headed for the port. This time we were in luck and managed to catch the evening ferry back to Banjul. We found a place to sit high up on deck with a good view of the sun setting over the ocean. Belle sat on my lap and I heard her talking to Hush.

'Wasn't that a nice day?' she whispered, before nodding off to sleep.

George Bernard Shaw is a human-rights barrister who was called to the Bar by the Honourable Society of the Inner Temple in 1997. After practising in the UK for many years, he returned to Ghana where he now works. He divides his time between his Accra  office and his beachside home where he owns a 150-foot-long, brightly painted fishing canoe. He has declined all offers of a trip out to sea.

A Winter in Menorca

Kirsty Fergusson

23 April 2001

It's time to go. For three-and-a-half months my three youngest
children and I have been living on a windy, blue and white island in
the Mediterranean – residing, working and going to school in a place
we have all come to think of as home. Now the cases are packed, the
farewells have been said and in a few hours we will be climbing aboard
the ferry that will take us to Barcelona on the first leg of the long
journey home to Dorset by land and sea.

We came to escape the British winter and find a bit of breathing
space, post-divorce. In the event, we found a great deal more than any
of us had anticipated.

Our artist friend, Ken, had said a strange thing when we arrived.
'You'll find Menorca an oddly confrontational place to live,' he said.
'I don't mean that the people are confrontational; it's the island that
challenges you. It's a bit like living in New York: you have to live
with it, rather than in it. Maybe it's because it's an island; maybe it's
to do with the extreme winds we have to live with; maybe it's the
intransigence of the landscape. I don't know. But live with it, Kirsty,
and you'll never want to leave.'

Well, it's true, I don't want to leave – and the children feel the
same way. Of course, we've missed our friends and family, our animals

and every soggy square inch of our lovely Dorset valley, so our homecoming will be as joyful as it will be noisy. But – and this is the 'Big But'– when you have lived in a place you love, a part of your heart gets left behind. And this despite it getting attached to the strangest – and seemingly most insignificant – things. Anyway, according to our friends we'll be back. Oh yes, they say, with knowing looks, you'll be back. And not just for your holidays, either.

Mind you, it's not been easy all the time. My thirteen-year-old son has found it tough going being the only English boy at his secondary school in Mahon, which lies a bus ride away from our clifftop suburb of Es Castell.

'Mum, what does *guiri* mean?' he asked, flinging his rucksack down with venom, as he came in from school one day. 'It's my nickname; everyone calls me *guiri*.'

'It means foreigner,' I said, 'but they don't mean any harm. It's like us using "grockles" for the tourists in Dorset.' He sighed. 'But it means you don't belong, doesn't it?'

I knew what he meant. We weren't tourists, but we weren't residents either and our groping attempts to speak Spanish only served to emphasise our foreignness. We'd been on the island four weeks and the lady in the bread shop still hadn't smiled at me. I was going to Spanish classes two evenings a week, yet stringing a sentence together that I hadn't had time to prepare remained beyond me. The children seemed to be making rapid headway, yelling in Spanish at friends in the street all the things that kids always seem to be yelling at each other, but it was obviously a struggle for them to keep up in the classroom. 'I got sent out for dropping a pencil on the floor,' said my ten-year-old son cheerfully. 'It was quite nice actually, because it was all quiet in the corridor and I didn't have to listen to the teacher going on and on in Spanish.'

A day or two later I bravely attended a parents' evening at the school, sitting in my children's classroom while the term's activities were spelt out for our benefit. I strained my ears and concentrated, attempted to jot down dates and notes and felt ridiculously pleased when the teacher beamed at me for trying so hard. It lasted for just forty minutes. I don't know if I could have managed six hours of it without dropping my pencil in the hope of being sent outside. The teacher kissed me on both cheeks when I left.

Our clothing set us apart, too. While local children walked to school in attire designed for a particularly severe alpine winter, mine went in short sleeves and often shorts. Other mothers raised their eyebrows, made shivering gestures and tutted. The children were oblivious and – by English standards, anyway – it wasn't cold. '*Guiri*,' teased Clare, a friend of Ken's who has worked on the island for seven years and is completely fluent in both Spanish and Catalan. 'Only *guiris* wear shorts and T-shirts in March!' 'But according to the papers,' I objected indignantly, 'this is the hottest March since records began in 1856.' Clare tucked her chin into her woolly roll-neck sweater and grinned at me. '*Guiri*,' she repeated.

Meal times were a bit of an issue too. 'Don't mum, please!' said my younger two children as we stood at the meat counter, looking at the eviscerated rabbits and tiny bodies of thrushes. 'You can get chicken nuggets and frozen chips, honestly! They do sell them here.' But I was relentless and, having been loaned a copy of Carmen Puigvert's book *Traditional Menorcan Cooking*, I told them sternly that it was *sofrit* and *sobressada* from now on. With lots of the vegetables for which Menorca is famous: tiny aubergines and artichokes, peas and potatoes, French beans and tomatoes.

But after a few weeks I got bored with making *sofrit*, which is a melted mixture of onion, garlic, tomato and pepper to which meat or vegetables are added and cooked in an earthenware casserole. And the *sobressada* – a soft, spicy sausage – appealed to none of us very much. I ate it on toast, with honey for breakfast, like the book said, while the children stared at me over their bowls of Weetabix as though I were completely mad. It wasn't very nice. Most of the *sobressada* stayed in the fridge for several weeks, and although I grew quite fond of its presence there, it ended up as fishing bait. The sausage made one last appearance, however, in a skipping rhyme that my eight-year-old daughter had learned in the school playground. '*Sobressada, sobressada,*' she sang as she jumped, and then, not knowing the rest of the words, went on, 'Chi-cken nuggets and chips'.

As the days lengthened and the temperature rose we found our small world expanding as we made new friends. The older son found an ally and mate in an English boy who had grown up on the island and was bilingual. 'Do you have a nickname at school?' I heard my son ask his new friend while they booted a football around the beach. 'Yeah, it's *guiri*,' came the reply. The lady in the bread shop started to smile at me, and I even managed a phone call in Spanish with the Guardia Civil (police). We took the car on the ferry to Mallorca and drove into the mountains, visiting Deià and Valldemossa; we visited an enchanting garden that I was to write about near Pollença and returned to Alcúdia three days later to catch the ferry back to Menorca. It was an illuminating experience. 'I don't like it here,' said my daughter. 'Everyone speaks German and it's too big. I want to go home.' She meant home to Menorca. The boys agreed. 'Menorca's more…. homey,' they suggested, uncertain of what they were really trying to say.

* * *

1 August 2018

My children are grown-up now, and Bradt Travel Guides' invitation to submit a story for this anthology sent me searching through old archived files of stories I never submitted for publishing. So I'm remembering as I write – with all the filters and fancies of seventeen intervening years.

We didn't fly home; the transition would have been too startling, too immediate. Instead, we took the ferry to Barcelona, then a long bus ride to London and a train to Dorset. The idea was that the long, slow journey would give us all time to adjust: as the landscape outside the window transitioned from Mediterranean to northern European, so we would gradually let go of our island selves in order to settle back into our previous lives.

But how odd: what should have seemed familiar had now become strange, at least for a while. The milk that at first tasted peculiar in Menorca, meant that 'normal milk' – as the children called it and endlessly mourned during our stay overseas – now did not taste quite right. Without wanting to admit it, there were lots of things to which we had grown accustomed that would now and forever more provide an alternative point of reference.

The absence of school uniforms; the respect shown to elderly people, kissing and pinching cheeks by way of greeting; the colour of the sea; the late, late suppers; the little tortoises hiding under massive aloes in the garden; and the way that Catalan managed to say something about the place that English could not. *Tramuntana* described a wind that had kept us housebound for three days and smothered the windows in salt; a *migjorn* coated us in Saharan sand and made us long for the dry westerly *ponent*. In short, our absolutes had become relative and our vocabularies bigger, but for my children this loss of old certainties was initially troubling. So over the years we returned to the windy, blue and white island – not often, but enough to allow the difference to become normal, enough for them to belong in more than one place – and enough to prepare them for their future journeys into the unknown, together and alone.

Back in the eighties, **Kirsty Fergusson** exchanged a career in academia for a life of gardening, writing and travel, and now lives in southwest France. She is the author of Bradt Travel Guides' award-winning title in the Slow Travel series, *Cornwall and the Isles of Scilly*, and has also contributed to Bradt's anthology about solo travel, *Roam Alone*.

Bulgarian Lessons

Jonathan Campion

The world is very small when you're four. When I told my son that we were going to Bulgaria, he thought that it was at the end of a London bus route. And while taking Andrew to a little town in the Thracian Valley to meet my partner's family was a bigger step for us than journeys home on the 152, for him the experience of making friends in a new country turned out to feel just as comfortable.

The trip was Andrew's first without his mum. Not that he was anxious about going away. Pavlina and I were dreading waking him up before dawn for our flight. When morning came, he was waiting impatiently by the door with his rucksack before we had even brushed our teeth. Arriving in the Bulgarian capital of Sofia after a three-hour flight, Andrew hurried us through the airport and carried our bags to the taxi rank.

There were a couple of hours before our bus to Yambol; enough time for a bite at Zhenski Bazaar (the 'Women's Market') on the way. It's a true Balkan bazaar: old and open-air, loud and chaotic. Stalls are stacked with clothes and shoes, while tables are covered with baskets full of bulbous grapes, sweet peppers, ripe strawberries, glossy cherries, and lots more that the women working at the tables had plucked from their gardens that morning. Fresh food is an obsession in Bulgaria: even on a Thursday afternoon the place was packed.

At a café in the middle of the market, melting into scruffy leather sofas and eating rice pudding with cinnamon stirred in, we watched the world go by. Immersed in the new smells, caught up in the commotion, Andrew's eyes lit up. While Pavlina and I sipped fiendish Balkan espressos in paper shot glasses, he vaulted off the sofa and scurried up a nearby tall metal staircase for a better view.

Watching Andrew exploring fearlessly, curious about it all, made me think of my own first day in Bulgaria the year before. Staying in Sofia for work, I had been so self-conscious about not speaking the language that I didn't leave my hotel in the evenings.

From the market, we took a taxi to the bus station. The bus was as chaotic as the bazaar: passengers jostling for seats, shoving bags into every spare inch, restless at the prospect of a five-hour, cross-country slog. As we set off, old ladies bellowed into their phones to tell their families that they were on the way home. Then everyone opened snacks. It's a long road to the Thracian Valley; bottles of Zagorka and Kamenitza beer were flipped open too.

As the grey outskirts of the capital faded into the rugged greens and browns of Bulgaria's plains, another noise filled the bus: gentle snores coming from the head in my lap.

In Yambol that evening, Pavlina's mother (Lilyana) and stepfather (Bob), brought us home to a Bulgarian welcome: the aroma from a coffee pot warmed the apartment, and the living-room table was covered with plates of food. We had come for a double-celebration weekend: Lilyana's retirement party and her birthday. Gifts were exchanged. I gave Lilyana a scarf; she presented Andrew with a full set of new clothes and an autumn coat.

This part of Bulgaria once lay in a region known as Thrace, a land now shared with the northern parts of neighbouring Greece and

Turkey. Yambol is famous for its wine, made from delicious Mavrud grapes cultivated in Thracian vineyards – or often fermented at home. Lilyana toasted our arrival with both versions. Then it was Andrew's bedtime. Once Bob and Pavlina's father Dimitar had each fed me a tumbler of homemade *rakia*, Bulgaria's overpowering grape spirit, my bed was calling too.

Andrew's initiation the next morning was gentler. Over glasses of apple juice, Pavlina's two nieces, Ivayla and Lili, practiced their English on him. Andrew learned some Bulgarian words – and with them took a crash course in the country's culture. When you come home, you take off your shoes and put on some woolly slippers called *shushonki*. Before you take a first sip of drink, you say *nazdrave* ('to your health'). Instead of goodbye, it's *dovizhdane* ('until I see you again'). By the afternoon Andrew was proudly saying *haide* ('let's go!'), with a Yambol accent to boot.

When the children ran out of words, they still found a common language. Bulgarian kids play the piano and dance around to music videos. Bulgaria has toy cupboards with costumes, parks with playgrounds, cafés with ice cream. Bulgarians give hugs and kisses. Andrew made himself at home.

Watching Andrew and the girls playing, racking their brains to find things they had in common, I thought of the friendships I had refused by fixating on differences. A few years previously when I was studying near Moscow, some Russian students invited me to play volleyball with them. I felt my weak hits didn't fit in, so I slid away early, without saying goodbye. Too often we assume that other cultures are much different to ours. It takes children to notice what is familiar.

The next day Lilyana's friends came to the flat, and her retirement party began with another feast. The only rule of Bulgarian gatherings is to be yourself: there are neither pressures nor expectations. And so, guests in party frocks caught up with friends in pyjamas. People came late after work and started on the salad when everyone else was already on dessert. Wine glasses clinked against mugs of tea. Friends who had known each other for decades switched to their second language, so that the little boy from England could feel part of the celebration.

At the heart of this inclusiveness are children. They are sent to bed early on school nights, but always stay up late with their parents at weekends. When families get together – which, in Bulgaria, is every weekend – one child is appointed to look after the others. This child (*kaka* if a girl; *batko* for a boy) is usually the oldest, as they have to stay awake until the rest of the kids have crashed in the spare bedroom. An extra slice of cake is the reward for their night's work. This evening Andrew's *kaka* was Bella, the ten-year-old daughter of one of Lilyana's friends.

Strangers' hands appeared in front of Andrew's face to place bites of food in his mouth: *shopska* salad, sugar-dusted bread, pickled cucumber, strained yoghurt and *banitsa* (a cheese-filled pastry). Andrew didn't know what any of them were – yet devoured them trustingly. Seeing him embrace the new food without hesitation, I again thought back to my first time in Bulgaria. I had never heard of any of the dishes served in the cafés, so lived on cold pizza from street kiosks.

The celebration was about to move to a restaurant in the town. But it was already Andrew's bedtime. Just as our taxi arrived at Lilyana's apartment, his mum video-called, wanting to wish him goodnight. If she found out our plan – for him to party with us until Bella could lay him down on a pile of coats – he would never be allowed to come to Yambol again. But Andrew had an idea. Grinning like a Cheshire cat, he jumped into bed, tucking the blankets up to his chin to hide his party clothes. After a minute he yawned dramatically and said goodnight to his mum… so we could whisk him down the stairs and into the car.

It was 3 a.m. when Andrew really went to bed. After a second dinner, the restaurant's tables were pushed back to transform the dining area into a disco. The children did cartwheels on the dancefloor and, long past midnight, Ivayla and Bella helped Andrew into a handstand. This time I joined them: my son had shown me that it was time I followed his example for a change.

The next day we had to say *dovizhdane* and return home – but not before we had hatched plans for Pavlina's family to come to visit us as soon as they could. After our flight from Sofia landed, I took Andrew back to his mum on the 152 bus. I had never seen him so happy as with his unexpected new friends. Andrew had learned that Bulgaria isn't at the end of a London bus route. But he knows it isn't far.

Jonathan Campion is a writer based in Suffolk. In between journeys with Andrew and Pavlina, he has also travelled across Europe, Russia, the Caucasus and Central Asia, while working as a translator and wine/spirits analyst. Jonathan has written for *The Calvert Journal*, *Wisden Cricketers' Almanack*, and several travel magazines. His photography has been published too. He tweets ➤ @jonathancampion and his website is w jonathancampion.com.

The Castle of Misadventure

Mairi McCurdy

By the age of eighteen I was infected with the travel bug. My mother had gently encouraged me to take flight, nudging me into the world and setting me free. By my mid-forties, with a family of my own, wanderlust felt like a healthy kind of virus to be passing on. My husband Michel and I had started cautiously: holidays in the safe second homes of fellow families where travel cots, baby gates and emergency buggies were always on hand. But now that our daughters – Mia (nine) and Jana (seven) – were older, it seemed right to be trying something slightly more adventurous: touring Tuscany and Veneto under canvas (or rather, nylon).

The first Italian campsite was on a breathy, terraced hillside outside Monte Catini. Because our girls were big enough to accept invitations to play Uno at the pool within spitting distance of the tent or to hang out at the table-tennis table, I rarely saw them. Instead, I struggled with the daily hauling of dirty dishes to the wash house, the lingering for a tiny window of opportunity when the washing machine might finally be free, or the interminable wait for the toilet. Then there was cooking in the heat – a smeary, slippery exercise – and the sleeping mattress, which, at best, resembled a rather choppy waterbed.

The girls rolled their eyes at the very mention of a 'day trip'. This unwelcome suggestion would mean dragging themselves away from their new friends or from Enid Blyton's *Adventure Series*. The agreed compromise was to alternate: one day campsite, next day culture. In Florence, the humidity slowed the kids to a crawl: we couldn't even reach the end of the street without stopping for *una Coca* or an extortionately priced *gelato*. But this was *my* trip down memory lane and the girls were going to enjoy it whether they liked it or not.

So – to fed-up faces set upon slouching shoulders – I pointed out the piazzas through which I had cycled and fountains in which I had jumped while an ecstatic and energetic exchange student. But the Ponte Vecchio transpired to be a crowded bling-filled bore, where a dropped strawberry ice cream slopped a pink puddle upon medieval cobbles. Pisa didn't go any better – tickets to the leaning *campanile* were deemed too expensive and our 'holding-up-the-tower' photos were sabotaged by a forest of selfie-sticks.

Puccini's birthplace of Lucca, however, was a surprise hit – especially when a dazzling soprano and blind tenor enchanted us with *O Soave Fanciulla*. Within a week we were screaming our own version on the *autostrada* as we headed north to Venice. But after more heat and queuing and even more people, the mosaics in San Marco lost their lustre, while on the piazza the pigeon-police arrested any joyful plans to feed the birds. Tears were inevitable, and we succumbed to Aqualandia, 'Italy's number one water theme park'.

To be frank, camping had been tough. We were down to our very last pairs of everything. On the day we left Italy to head north towards Germany, emergency handwashing of our smalls was required. Underwear was duly pegged on an ingenious rack that Michel had designed to prevent our children being buried in an avalanche of luggage. I took my accustomed position in the passenger seat – the optimum place to fulfil my duties as sandwich-spreader and drink-provider – passing treats into the back where the girls listened to stories, read, slept or squabbled.

We made steady progress through the Alpine foothills of northern Italy and into Austria. Michel disappeared into a podcast, Mia returned to Blyton's *Castle of Adventure*, Jana sang to herself and I stared into the swelling landscape, recalling my very first foreign adventure, as an eighteen-year-old: Schloß Elmau.

This sumptuous Bavarian castle-hotel near Mittenwald in Garmisch-Partenkirchen provided both my first job and my inaugural overseas stint. I thought back to one particular weekend when, with a ponytailed guitar-player in tow, I hitched from the castle to Innsbruck and then on to Venice. On the roadside now, I smiled at a young couple hitch-hiking, their thumbs dropping at the sight of our bursting Berlingo. I could almost see myself standing with a cardboard sign, nowhere to stay and nothing but a few Deutschmarks in my pocket: anything seemed possible back then.

Schloß Elmau would be nearby, I thought. Maybe we could visit... but it had been a rather strange place. A cultural refuge for Germany's wealthiest. There were lectures and concerts: Yehudi Menuhin had played there once. At the weekly balls we 'helpers' put down our brushes and dusters to dance a quadrille with any lonely dukes or barons: all for a princely single Deutschmark per hour. I'd read that world leaders – including Obama, Merkl and Cameron – had met there in 2015 to thrash out issues concerning the global economy at a G7, and that now the hotel had been modernised with a swimming pool on the roof.

Back when I had polished the hallway, scandal oozed out of every crack. A disgruntled helper set fire to the tearoom and later ripped marble sinks from the walls with his bare hands. And, of course, there were the affairs and the outbreak of salmonella... Then there was the owner – a crazy old lady who lay bed-bound in one of the tower rooms and to whom nobody wished to take the lunchtime tray, but even as I polished the silver, sliced *Schwarzwälderkirschtorte* and hung up the furs of octogenarian Nazi widows, I'd been plotting my return to Garmisch.

'We could stop at Schloß Elmau and show the kids where I worked,' I said suddenly.

'It's a bit out of the way,' replied Michel.

'Oh,' I said, the sheen of my spontaneity dulled. Wailing from the backseat reinforced a brutal return to reality. a paper cut from the evil Enid. Handbag. Steri-wipes and plasters. A smeary chocolate biscuit dried the stubborn tears, and all was quiet again. I glanced back: one child cradling a finger, two little heads bumping against the window, headphones on. I looked at myself: skirt littered with pieces of bread; bags of apples, cucumber, tomatoes and breadsticks stacked around my feet, Swiss-Army knife sticky with cheese. Elmau was another life. Another person.

Driving through rippling pasture, icy summits rose on either side while chalets sprouted from a verdant carpet, petunias cascading from their window boxes. It was like Dorothy opening the door on Oz: a technicolour dreamscape urging me to leap from the passenger seat, fling crumbs and cheese-rind from my lap, run up the nearest slope and sing...

'We're actually not far from Mittenwald,' said Michel, changing his tune.

My heart leapt. 'Girls, would you like to see where Mummy worked once? The castle – the posh place, remember?'

'Can we get ice cream?'

'I'm sure they have ice cream.'

Family permission to visit was secured, but there was a problem. Our way was blocked: 'Privatstraße' read an unrelenting sign. A round-faced man with impressive facial hair and cash box informed us that driving up this forested private road would cost us. But after nearly thirty years and a journey of unfolding memories, I was prepared to pay. Sunlight glinted through the bars of trees while anticipation prowled in my belly. Then darkness thinned, and the expanse of a rolling Bavarian meadow opened: vivid green, studded with wild flowers. After three decades without it, the sweep to the castle took my breath away. To think that this had once been my every day.

Parking up, we took pictures while the kids skipped through pasture, picking asters and gentians to weave into my hair as we sat on the very bench that had supported the world's great leaders. 'You should go in,' said Michel. But we'd both seen the unequivocal, off-putting signs. 'Car park strictly for residents.' 'Private.' 'Café and restaurant for residents only.'

'No chance. They'll turn me away.'

'You scrubbed their stairs and stacked their plates. Surely they'll sell you a coffee!' I looked at my greasy skirt and chipped toenail varnish. Then ignored them. 'Sod it,' I decided. 'There's no harm in trying. Coming, girls?'

I marched uphill to the castle, kids running through the long grass, tickling each other with long stems, while Michel waited below. Crunching over the courtyard, I passed BMWs, Aston Martins and Rolls Royces.

'Madam, may I help you?' I smiled at the concierge who pointed me to reception where a slick young man shuffled papers and a red-nailed receptionist tapped at a screen.

'How can we be of assistance?' asked the man, features rigid.

'*Guten Tag.*' I spoke in German. 'I've come from Ireland with my family. I was a chambermaid here, a *Helferin*, almost thirty years ago. I'd very much like to show my children where I worked.'

'I see.'

'Our rooms were in the cellar. We earned one Deutschmark an hour...'

'Things have changed since then.' He looked at his colleague with raised eyebrows. 'One moment, please.' He punched a few numbers into the telephone and muttered inaudibly down the receiver. He turned to me, this time with a slight smile.

'You may tell your family to come. They may bring the car to the front of the hotel.'

'Oh, thank you. Thank you very much,' I said, delighted and somewhat surprised. I waved gleefully to Michel and watched as our silver Berlingo snaked its way up to the car park.

'Did you ask about the ice cream?' Michel inquired with a smile as he climbed out of the car. The concierge appeared, hand outstretched. Michel was unclear whether to shake it or put money in it. The man pointed to the keys Michel was holding. Nervously handing over the car keys, we turned to the castle.

The girls were ahead of us, cautious and reverent for the first time in days. Michel took my hand and we entered the cool marble of Schloß Elmau.

As we made our way to the terrace, the ghosts of eighteen-year-old girls sang Christmas carols, wiped bannisters, brushed stairs, polished floors, folded towels, served and danced. Lazing in the sunshine, we played the elite for an hour, pretending we knew how the other half lived. The ice cream and the coffee cost an eyewatering fifty euros, prompting the girls to lick out every last drop then – to make absolutely sure – to rub round the glass with a little finger.

The majestic Wetterstein mountains were a glistening backdrop for my girls who twirled and cartwheeled. We reclined into the falling of the day as I spoke of the cellar, the fire, the hitch-hiking, the singing and the admission that this place wasn't us and that a coffee was as much as I would ever want here...

And then a flash of far more recent memory stopped me dead. The *pants*. The pants in the back window of the car. Michel had handed the keys of our Berlingo to the concierge, an employee parking BMWs and Aston Martins for a living... And we had given him our smelly, crumb-filled vehicle, bursting with sweaty tent and floppy airbeds, the excuse-for-a-rubbish-bin overflowing in the front, and – in unimpeded view – a makeshift washing line with a pretty selection of adult and children's underwear, swinging merrily in time with our deep, resounding laughter.

Belfast-born writer **Mairi McCurdy** began writing seriously whilst living abroad. Her experiences in Europe and Asia lie at the heart of her short stories and young-adult fiction. Since returning to live in County Down (Northern Ireland) she has found inspiration from the majestic Mourne mountains where she lives with her husband and daughters. She is completing a novel set in Germany at the time of the fall of the Berlin Wall.

Being Explorers, Having an Adventure... and Going to School

Celia Dillow

My three lovely boys looked uncomfortable. They had put on socks and shoes for the first time in seven weeks, plus long trousers, shirts and ties. But it was not the Buenos Aires heat that provoked their discomfort.

All three were strangely mute during an edgy breakfast. When it was time to go, nine-year-old Matt headed across the field to the junior school and the two eldest (Will, fourteen and Bobby, eleven) walked the fifty metres to the senior-school quad where they would be sorted and sifted into tutor groups. Wary and watchful, they merged with the crowd but were not part of it. I joined the milling parents who were gradually filling the auditorium for the opening *acto* of the new academic year. Last year's prize-winning students paraded with flags, and we stood to sing the school song and, hands on hearts, the rousing but unknowable Argentine national anthem. The air was hot: new school uniforms stuck to nervous bodies; parents fanned themselves.

The start-of-term ceremony, with its rallying words and national pride, was hard to follow; it must have been impenetrable for the boys.

How could we have prepared them for this? How would they ever fit in? As we left the hall I saw both older boys and my mummy-heart was broken all over again. Bobby looked close to tears, his blue eyes large and wild in his pale face. Will, so resistant to this move anyway, was dark with anger. The holidays were definitely over.

I walked home slowly and sat at my desk. This was the first day of my new life too. I picked at the ends of the work I had left unfinished in December, before we moved continents. For a couple of hours I lost myself in something. But little bubbles of worry kept rising, forcing me to think of the boys, worry about them, pray for them. In the end I found myself sitting and staring. I felt unhinged, powerless and sick. They were doing such a difficult thing and I could not do it for them.

The decision weighed on my mind.

Eighteen months ago we had decided to move to South America. As newlyweds, that continent had conquered us and changed our lives; we had brought up our boys on tales of faraway. They had been spellbound by our stories of eagles and hummingbirds and armadillos. They had drooled at the thought of steaks the size of their heads. They knew where the rhea laid her eggs and what a penguin colony sounded like. They wanted to see, taste and feel it themselves. So one ragged Christmas, we returned to the wide horizons and endless possibilities of the continent that had made us. We sold up, packed up and went to teach at a school in Argentina.

The establishment was on a gated, guarded campus, twelve miles south of Buenos Aires. It looked like an English boarding school, with rugby posts and cricket nets. There were some mellow old buildings, modern science labs and art rooms, and a tiny chapel. But there were also parakeets shrieking in the palm trees and caracara hawks turning in the heat haze above the playing fields. It was not

England and settling in took resilience and determination. Early days were spent achieving a list of small, prosaic triumphs: the first successful journey into our local town in the new car, without getting lost; our first trip to the supermarket; a visit to the bank to open an account; a chat with the butcher and baker; finding a barber and a dentist; buying school uniforms.

By the end of January we felt brave enough to take a holiday. We drove the 250 miles south to Mar de las Pampas, one of a string of beach resorts on the South Atlantic coast. It was the boys' first real glimpse of wild Argentina – and we wanted them to love it. The road south was fast and straight. On the rural stretches there was exotic wildlife to spot: flamingos, ibises and spoonbills. There were rheas in groups and *tijeretas* (fork-tailed flycatchers) on telephone wires. Everything was new and our senses were overloaded. We stopped at the roadside for *empanadas* (small pasties) and *choripan* (hot dogs) and taught the boys to wind up the windows quickly to avoid the smell of roadkill skunks. The journey passed without too much bickering from the back rows.

At the beach the air was scented with pine and eucalyptus. The roads were sandy tracks; pretty cabins of logs and stone huddled under the trees. The town centre was made of timber walkways that meandered through the woods. The shops were like tree houses. Late into the soft, austral night the place was busy with families browsing the boutiques and choosing a place to eat. Hot pine sap mingled with the aroma of meat roasting on an *asado* barbecue. There were strings of tiny lights in the trees and the constant sound of a thousand wind chimes.

A tall dune and a beach of white sand swept south towards the end of the world. Terns fished along the fringes. We baked in the sun while the boys experimented with sandboards. In the afternoons we shopped for handicrafts and ate *dulce de leche* ice cream. The boys were delighted with everything and really did eat steaks the size of their heads.

However, our lives had become too closely entwined during that extraordinary winter – one that had become summer thanks to twelve hours in an aeroplane. The boys argued with one other and with us, throwing their weight around and refusing to co-operate. Everyone fell out. Our new life and idyllic surroundings did not mask our individual and collective nervousness about the future. At precisely the ages that boys were pre-programmed to start questioning our boundaries and values, we had plunged them and ourselves into a life where even we adults did not know the rules. Without a support network of friends to call on, we were going to have to rely on each other in an abnormal way.

And so we returned to the city on the quest for some routine. We needed to go back to school.

The waiting – on the afternoon of that first day at the new school – was interminable. First through the door at half-past four was Matt. Smiling and jolly, he had made lots of friends and liked his teacher. Bobby arrived next. He cried when he saw me and admitted that it was hard. But he was tough as well as sensitive. He knew he had to make it work and, after a drink and a snack, he looked brighter and told some good tales. The doors crashed again, kicked wide by Will's huge feet. I noticed that his pristine new uniform already looked lived in. He acted cool but gave me a quick smile, 'It was alright Mum, stop worrying'. Eating their way through a loaf's worth of toast and jam, the boys were soon comparing notes and laughing about mistakes they had made: who had what for lunch; which teachers they shared; who spoke some Spanish; did anyone understand anything?

I was light-headed with relief.

We fell quickly into the rhythm of the term. In order to survive, the boys quickly learnt all the swear words – and the words for foodstuffs. What more did boys need? One evening I heard one of them snarl, '*Vos sos una sacapuntas!*' Deciding to clamp down, I turned quickly on the guilty party and was surprised when they dissolved into giggles. 'Mum, he called me a pencil sharpener!' It sounded like a bad word to me.

Life at school had its own rhythm, bound by bells and timetables. But at every break we headed out of the city and across the *pampa*, through small towns and on to vast *estancias*. We even drove a thousand miles in a weekend to see condors in Córdoba – one youngster coming so close that we could count individual feathers and hear the wind rustling under its endless wings. The autumn sun shone, the air was fresh, and it was good to be away from the capital. Perhaps because their parents were so relaxed, the boys were considerate company – remaining cheerful despite long hours in the car and keen to explore with us.

And so we travelled. We criss-crossed the country in a series of ambitious road trips. We followed brick-red roads northeast to the famous waterfalls of Iguazú. We made a night-time safari through the Chaco forest in pursuit of the tapir. And we searched for monkeys in the dripping cloud forest of Calilegua. We all loved the high and bleak Andean provinces of the north and west. We returned often to visit Patagonia's spectacular wildlife. We slid on unsealed roads, got stuck in the mud and changed tyres in thunderstorms. During those journeys, we forged bonds that would bend and buckle with the strain of growing up together. The boys learnt that their parents were brave and scared and imperfect; we learnt to look again through young, curious eyes full of wonder.

So, as we clattered towards the end of the first year, we could not believe how brilliant and tough our boys had been. They had made friends, joined teams and crunched verb tables. They had all confided that they thought their new life was pretty cool. They had learned how to be guests in a foreign land and how it felt to be an outsider. We had ripped out our roots, packed ourselves up and travelled a very long way together – physically and emotionally. Everyone had survived. Without a doubt we had all been enchanted. The unknowable, alien land of Argentina had charmed and challenged us with her unruly, raucous ways and staggering landscapes. We had started to feel at home. We toasted our brave decision and our courageous children – but, even then, had no idea quite how much braver we would all have to be in the year that followed.

Celia Dillow spent five years in South America. It changed everything. Now settled in southwest Britain, she reads and writes about the magic and mystery of those faraway southern lands. She is a specialist dyslexia teacher during term time and a traveller, writer, birdwatcher and hiker during the holidays.

Chinese Blessings

Marie Noonan

L ike all the best adventures, our visit to Jinghong, a tropical city in southwest China's Yunnan province, was almost accidental. My husband and I were travelling independently around China with our daughter (Caoimhe, aged twelve) and two sons (Aonghus, eleven, and Cormac, nine). Whilst we had moments of mutiny from the three children and 'comfort' became a relative term, we also had tremendous fun and great laughs.

We were in Xinjie to see the rice terraces. Flicking through the guide book, Aonghus's attention was grabbed by an account of a 'water-splashing festival' in Jinghong to celebrate the Dai New Year. Could we go? The timing was right and, consulting a map, it didn't seem very far.

Big mistake.

The road leaving Xinjie wound like a corkscrew, granting us views from every direction of the famous rice terraces as they bathed in a dawn glow. Workers stood in knee-deep water, planting and weeding in an eternal back-breaking slog. After six hours on the rattling bus, our own backs were also feeling the pressure, especially when we discovered that we had only covered a tiny part of the journey.

It was about thirty-six hours later when we finally staggered from the bus in Jinghong. We had (just about) survived four connections and a mad scramble for tickets that involved much shouting, pushing and hand-wringing. We had snatched a few hours rest in some unknown hill town, napping on soft beds with red satin throws and a party of mice in the roof. We had subsisted on fried rice and dumplings then chewed on the dust that filled the bus on the unpaved sections that amounted to more than half the journey.

Fortunately, the swirling dust had only partly veiled the glorious scenery, which included high mountains, dense forests, fast-flowing rivers and deep gorges. Until that bus ride, we had never conceived that China was so beautiful. We gawped at enormous horizontal concrete pillars that had been erected in valiant efforts to prevent erosion of some hillsides. At one point, showers of pebbles cascaded on to the bus roof like hailstones. Around the next corner, the road was blocked by a landslide; two yellow bulldozers did what they could.

The dust had also turned the routine spitting of bus passengers into a symphony of coughs and croaks. I winced as a man seated in front of me hawked an enormous gob of phlegm through an open window. Cormac and Aonghus had no such qualms: instead, they challenged each other to see who could spit further.

As we trundled along, the bus stopped regularly to let people on and off: women with shopping baskets, old but sprightly men and schoolchildren. Different in so many ways yet with one thing in common: everyone was clutching a mobile phone, yakking away loudly and never once losing reception despite the remote, mountainous surroundings.

'Are we really there?' Caoimhe lifted her eyes from a Harry Potter book to stare at Jinghong's wide streets, which were bedecked with vats of pink and red flowers and marshalled by a regiment of palm trees that stomped through the centre. The city seemed to have entered three-o'clock slump – a sleeping-beauty spell hung in the thick hot air. The collective lethargy infected us as we stepped off the bus. My eyes flickered and my legs were rubbery as if walking in a swimming pool. We were hot, tired and very cranky. But recovery was at hand in the shape of a café serving Western food. The kids decided that two days on a bus might even have been worth it for the better-than-homemade chocolate brownies we devoured. We found accommodation in a grubby guest house whose main advantage was its location – across the road from our new favourite café.

The water festival ran over three days. There were fireworks, dragon-boat racing on the Mekong River and parades by ethnic groups in traditional dress. The entire riverbank was chocka with stalls selling clothes, shoes, flowers and all kinds of food. Some of the edibles hailed straight from the river – Mekong moss transpired to be a dried seaweed. Fish barbecued on skewers, strange meats and baskets of small speckled eggs enticed the hungry. A camel with red flowers tucked behind its ears plodded by with two grinning girls on his hump. A bare-chested flame thrower juggled four fiery sticks, flinging them high into the air.

Some of the stalls offered games. Cormac was determined to have a go at one, hoping to win a teddy bear or a can of Coke. He closed an eye, took aim and flung a ball at some bottles and cans arranged on makeshift shelving. There was a groan from the crowd when he missed. He lined up again, tongue between lips in concentration, and threw. A bottle tumbled from its perch. It was 'whisky', the first of three bottles Cormac won that day. That he managed to exchange the trio of moonshine for a single can of Coke speaks volumes for the quality of the alcohol.

Caoimhe, meanwhile, dared her brother to try some barbecued bamboo worms – small and green but no longer wiggly. Aonghus picked one from the pile on the banana-leaf plate, sniffed and brought it to his mouth. 'It's delicious! Crunchy outside but airy inside… like a big Rice Krispie.' He licked his fingers as the crowd laughed.

In 'one-child' China, we were as much of a sideshow as any flame thrower. Staring in China is not only culturally acceptable but as natural as breathing. We attracted a lot of attention simply by being a family with three children. We got used to people approaching us and miming that they wanted to be photographed with us. Our faces ached from smiling.

We might have been at a water-splashing festival, but the throwing of water was confined to the third and final day. The children prepared by honing their bargaining skills, buying water pistols which were for sale on every corner. Unfortunately, they made the mistake of using our large, scowling landlord as target practice. We didn't need a translator to glean that our now-bellowing landlord was threatening to evict us. Given that the city was crammed with revellers eager to take our rooms, there was nothing for it but to haul the kids in front of Mr Grumpy and grovel. The boys joined hands and bowed in a universal gesture of apology. We were allowed to stay.

In the Dai language, Jinghong means 'City of the Dawn'. This was most apt, for early morning – with its fresh, pure air – proved the most pleasant time of day in this tropical city. On the third morning of the festival, I stepped outside the guest house at about 7 a.m. and, without the slightest warning, was swiftly drenched. The shock of cold water thrown from a balcony overhead left me breathless – for a second – and then screaming. I looked up at a young woman who waved an empty pink basin at me. Cold water trickled down my back as I stumbled back inside the door, slamming into Aonghus, who was on my heels. 'Great! It's started. Get the guns!' He turned and ran upstairs, shouting at the top of his voice.

The idea behind splashing water was to wash away the previous year's demons and usher in the happiness and good fortune of the Dai New Year. We stepped onto the street, moving cautiously and remaining vigilant. Nevertheless, within minutes all five of us were saturated, surrounded by hordes of grinning Chinese determined to wish us luck and happiness – by soaking us even more. We were blessed by kids holding water guns, basins of water were thrown at us from the roof and passing trucks crammed with people doused us. Everyone was sopping but we were wetter than most. Through this liquid mayhem, I spotted a fire truck careering down the street with its hose aimed at us.

'Take cover. I think we're the fire!' I shouted as we dodged behind a life-size ornamental elephant decorated with garlands of flowers. Water whooshed over the elephants and landed on us like a personal thunderstorm. 'We need more ammunition.' Caoimhe, who had the best aim, shook her almost empty gun. 'And bigger guns.'

The price of guns had more than tripled since the previous day but the street vendors were nevertheless doing brisk business in all sorts of 'weapons', basins, saucepans and buckets. The streets were closed to traffic and most shops and restaurants were boarded up – whether to allow their employees to partake in the festivities or to prevent their premises becoming waterlogged.

People of all ages ran laughing through the streets to the sound of beating drums, Chinese chimes and raucous screaming. With empty guns and basins, we dodged down a little alley into a courtyard where an elderly lady sat alone on a bench. She pointed to two taps. The air was light with the scent of frangipani and the chirping of birds. The woman dipped her slender fingers in a little blue porcelain bowl that lay upon her lap and sprinkled three or four drops of water on each of us. A true blessing in a tranquil haven.

Eventually, we braved it down to the main square, working as a team using tactics we had only ever seen in TV thrillers. The previous morning, we had visited the same square to watch the ritual morning exercises. In silent harmony, rows of people performed a series of graceful movements like the unfolding of a flower to the morning light.

Today could not have been more different. There was screaming chaos and hysterical laughter. People jostled each other to fill water pistols and basins from ornamental fountains and ponds. A bevy of uniformed gardeners wearing plastic coats blew whistles to prevent people trampling the flower beds. They were wasting their breath. One gardener gave up and decided to join in the fun. He stripped off his waterproofs and, with a gap-toothed smile, upturned a golden urn brimming with water over my head. The kids made sure that he was thoroughly blessed for this generous act.

'The Mekong must be nearly dry.' My husband nodded towards four trucks, laden with water barrels, coming from the direction of the river. We were now sitting on the upstairs veranda of the only restaurant that we could find open – a refuge with a view. We watched other foreigners squelching up the stairs, most with wizened, wrinkled skin from the incessant dousing. Our three children patrolled like urban snipers, refuelling from the bathroom and laughing at the kids on the street who threw water balloons up at them.

At three o'clock, a huge gong reverberated from the city centre and drums rolled to signal the end of the water splashing for another year. The city was no longer a huge, aquatic theme park. The kids groaned. The five of us stood together for a while, looking down at the wet streets with big grins on our faces. Two full days of travel had been a tiny price to pay for such an experience. Despite the drenching – or maybe because of it – we never felt luckier in our lives.

Marie Noonan lives in Co Waterford, Republic of Ireland, working as a medical scientist. She loves science, the outdoors and travel. She was very fortunate to spend a year travelling with her family around South America, Asia and Russia in 2008. Marie has read some of her memoir and fiction pieces on radio and was shortlisted for the *Irish Times* Amateur Travel Writer of the Year in 2015.

Kidding Around

NATURE VS NURTURE

Fun and Games Drive

Mike Unwin

'Daddy, do leopards roll in *every* animal's wee?'

The sing-song query cut through the African night, above the insect thrum, the hyena whoops and the camera shutter fusillade of the four other guests. The young leopard cavorting in our headlights froze, eyeballing us intently.

'Yes,' I whispered, when the cat at last looked away, trying frantically to hush my young inquisitor. 'I mean no. Probably. Now just watch, darling. We have to be very quiet – remember?'

It was summer 2006 in Zambia's South Luangwa National Park. My wife and I had upped sticks to the bush with our four-year-old daughter Flo for a three-month stint as conservation volunteers. Excursions with the upmarket local safari operators were generally beyond our means but we had managed to blag the odd freebie and now, for the first time, had brought Flo with us on a night drive. Mindful of the 'no under-12s' policy adopted by most lodges, we'd promised that our daughter would be no trouble and had briefed her exhaustively on the need for good behaviour, bribing her with sweets as required.

To be fair, she *had* been good so far. Hardly a squeak. But the leopard was the tipping point. It wasn't the animal itself that set her off but rather our guide's thrilling revelation about its behaviour. It turned out that the cat's rolling around – disporting itself with feline abandon – was, in fact, a ploy to mask its own scent in a dowsing of fresh antelope urine. Imagine that! An animal *rolling in wee*!

Now that the cat was out of the bag – so to speak – Flo's curiosity knew no bounds and, despite my whispered admonishments, her questioning pursued its own remorseless logic.

'Do leopards eat ducks?' she asked, slipping off my lap to grill our guide directly. 'Er... well, not usually,' came the game reply. A long pause followed. 'But I suppose they could,' he added. And then, turning to his clients: 'You see, the leopard is a remarkably versat...'

'So,' interrupted Flo, 'do leopards roll in duck wee?'

* * *

By now, we had learned to brace ourselves for the unexpected. Our route to Zambia had taken us via a self-drive safari in South Africa's Kruger Park, where 'Hate giraffes! Giraffes are boring!' had been an early shot across the bows.

'But giraffes are your favourite,' I had pleaded, trying to stem her tears. I knew she loved giraffes. How could she not? She had grown up on cuddly lions, happy hippos and cheeky meerkats. All her alphabet books ended in 'zebra'. Now, at last, I was showing her the real thing: forget all those toys and DVDs; forget *Giraffes Can't Dance*: the living, breathing, five-metre-tall reality was now looming over us – almost visibly affronted by our unimpressed daughter.

But such disappointments, I now realised, were my problem. Back in the UK, planning this trip, I had long anticipated Flo's first game-drive as a curtain-raiser moment; the spark that would ignite in her the same lifelong obsession that had claimed her father. To my adult mind, the giraffe was more than just an animal: it embodied the untamed allure of an entire continent. But Flo was unencumbered by such baggage. She was simply a tired four-year-old trapped in a hot car. The protracted I-spy game had long since run its course and now nothing, not even a Little Mermaid at the next waterhole, would raise a smile. When could she get out and run around? When could she have an ice cream?

Happily, we adapted. We quickly learned that there is only so long you can imprison a four-year-old in a vehicle, no matter what's outside the window, and that it is pointless waxing lyrical about wilderness unless there's a bit of it you can poke, chase or scribble on. Our drives became shorter. We gave up the relentless Big Five pursuit and instead stopped whenever Flo spotted something that grabbed her, whether oxpeckers whispering secrets into an impala's ear or an enormous steaming pile of 'very rude' elephant poo. We adjusted our itinerary to her needs, incorporating plenty of running-about time and picnic-site stops, where there was endless delight in fending off thieving glossy starlings, and a safari-in-miniature of tracks to follow and seed pods to shake, rattle and roll.

Meanwhile, we found undeniable relief in being able to eschew the usual anxious game-park agenda: all those pre-dawn departures and waterhole stakeouts. We could relax as the other vehicles chased their quarry over the horizon: childcare had given us a get-out clause. And, as so often happens when you take your foot off the gas, unexpected rewards followed – such as the African wild dog that chased an avalanche of impala from a roadside thicket as we were busy counting squirrels.

* * *

By the time we reached Zambia, we had all wised up a little. This was just as well, because our new home – on the banks of the Luangwa River – was crawling with wildlife. The challenge now was not so much how to keep Flo entertained by animals but more how to keep her out of their way. Elephants and hippos had us penned indoors after dark, hyenas rummaged through the camp dump, and the local leopard left her pugmarks on our back step. Our daily lectures exhorted Flo *never* to look under logs (snakes), approach the water's edge (crocs) or wander out of our sight (pretty much anything).

But she soon learned the ropes from her bush-wise pals on camp and quickly beame very blasé. 'Carry on, daddy!' she urged during a bedtime story, as I tailed off mid-sentence at the telltale munching of a jumbo outside our bathroom window. The Gruffalo was, at that point, a far more compelling beast than any real-life marauding pachyderm.

With game-viewing no longer the focus, the true value of our experience became clear. The bush was both playground and classroom. During free time we would poke around camp, luring ant-lion larvae from their pits with a grass blade and extracting millipede remains from a civet midden. Mopane seeds were for threading on a necklace, elephant tracks were for hopscotch and vervet monkeys were for mimicking. And, after dark, bush noises were simply an invitation to join in: Flo treated us to loud demonstrations of just how the mechanical *prrrp* of an African scops owl differed from the plaintive *peeu-peeu-peeu* of a pearl-spotted.

With interest came knowledge, and with knowledge the questions got harder. When, for instance, I explained how the warthogs bolting from us were holding their tails aloft in order more easily to follow one another, Flo immediately queried why the one at the back bothered to join in. A good point.

In turn, the uncensored natural world offered an ideal parental context in which to broach tricky subjects such as sex and death. And juvenile sensibilities turned out to be surprisingly robust – as we discovered later on that same night drive, when lions began dismembering a puku just metres from our vehicle.

'Is it dead, Daddy?' came a small, tear-stained voice, above the snarling and splintering of bone. 'Yes, I'm afraid so,' I replied, in sombre tones, struggling to shield her from the carnage. 'But don't be sad. Just think: if lions didn't catch antelopes, then baby lions would soon get hungry. And anyway, there are lots more antel…'

'But I wanted to see them *kill* it!'

* * *

Today, years later, friends ask how much our daughter remembers of that distant summer. It's now hard to separate fact from imagination. She claims, for example, that her favourite animal was a honey badger, even though she never saw one. But she can still reel off the calls of hippo and baboon (and, of course, African scops owl) without a moment's hesitation. Ultimately, does it matter what she can recall? While we adults are totting up our experience in a trophy cabinet of anecdotes and selfies, children simply absorb theirs and move on. Meanwhile its sediment filters slowly down, becoming the bedrock of who they will be.

The winter after our return from Africa, back home in Sussex, Flo stopped me during a muddy walk through our local woods and pointed out the paw prints of a large dog.

'Look dad!' she exclaimed. 'Hyena!'

Wrong, I thought. But not bad.

Mike Unwin is a writer of travel and nature books for adults and children. His Bradt titles include *100 Bizarre Animals* and *Southern African Wildlife*. His many other books include *Migration* (Bloomsbury) and *The Enigma of the Owl* (Yale). He won 'Travel Writer of the Year 2013' (British Guild of Travel Writers) and 'Nature Writer of the Year 2000' (*BBC Wildlife*), Mike writes regularly for the *Telegraph*, *The Independent*, *Travel Africa* etc.

Travel from the Doorstep

Nicola Chester

There is not a passport between us, in our family of five. Our three children (the eldest is 17) have yet to board a plane and fly anywhere. Yet last night, we saw four of the five species of owl resident in the UK – all within a mile of home.

We travel. Mostly, it has to be said, circling away from the doorstep in repeated arcs of a few miles or so, hare-like, haring about – as many families do. But we know our wild neighbours intimately and getting to know them is our first mission whenever we arrive anywhere.

Travel for us has always been on a tight budget. We often camp and when we are there, we explore our new temporary home from the doorstep (or awning) on foot, as freely (and cheaply) as possible.

Once, we camped in two small tents to give the children a greater sense of independence (and us a little peace). Only, we left one of the tents behind. The sight of all five of us and our collie dog leaving the two-man tent in quick succession the following morning caused a great deal of hilarity for our fellow campers among the Cumbrian hills.

Another time, we camped on a Welsh clifftop after a heatwave broke with a vengeance. Within hours, our tent blew down, the wind-up lantern hanging from the apex swinging wildly as a ship's bell before hitting me in the face at midnight. Yet, huddled in the car before the wind rocked us back to sleep, the storm blew through, leaving a washed-clean, star-filled sky, and we watched the first Perseid meteors fall through the sweep of the lighthouse beam from St Ann's.

My elder daughter has developed the habit of wild swimming to really immerse herself in a new place, whatever the season. My son likes to get the new mud of a place ingrained as soon as possible, disappearing off with map and mountain bike. Together we greet after-dark bin-raiding badgers and barbecue-licking foxes. We make a point of pointing these things out to others who might not have noticed, or celebrating them with locals, striking up conversations with strangers.

These are our real passports to place. Through the wild things that live where we merely visit, we have learned to notice more, and on a deeper level.

We travelled to Scotland on the proceeds of a book I wrote about otters, clutching an ambitious list of animals we'd like to see. The Glen Orchy mountain range filled the windows of the white croft cottage that was to be our home for the next week.

With a rucksack each, compass and map, we walked from the doorstep to the summit of Beinn na Sroine, the mountain behind the house. We left in warm sunshine that bookended a week of mizzle. It's a wonder we could move at all. Everywhere the family looked, we saw something new. The small, dark, velvety flight of Scotch Argus butterflies. A path imprinted by the feet of high-altitude water voles. There were red squirrel, wildcat, pine marten and golden eagle in these forests, and we thrilled to think of it.

We cleared the treeline with a sense of achievement. Rosie, just seven, was indefatigable in the lead. Below us, a corrie lake sparkled brilliance and the wide River Orchy snaked round its own hairpin bends with the blackness of a race track. On the open mountain, the path expired and the children struck out confidently on a compass bearing to the summit, like the good scouts they are. We stopped for lunch just as the expected weather closed in. We pulled on waterproofs and watched as the moor flared into radiance and small rainbows appeared around and below us. Then the sun disappeared for the week.

As it began to rain, the view changed and changed again, disappearing then reappearing. Walls emerged out of nowhere and granite boulders became sheep became boulders. Thinking I'd spotted the triangulation point, I lifted the binoculars – but with something of a shock, what I focussed on leapt up on broad, wide wings and vanished into the cloud. 'What's that?' I cried. Nobody else saw it. Its sheer size meant it could only have been a golden eagle. If, indeed, it was there at all. 'Was that…?' I faltered.

With the summit reached, my husband altered tack so we began our descent, straight down the mountain. Until this point, I'd been content (and lazy) enough to follow, marvelling at how well the children could navigate and orient themselves. Now a little, nagging voice came back to me, from when I had first properly travelled, with my own passport, aged eighteen. I'd gone native, living with cowboys and cowgirls on a ranch in Canada's Rocky Mountains. Occasionally, we'd meet members of the Tsuut'ina Indian First Nation community. An elder, intrigued by my British accent, offered me two pieces of advice. The first, that yarrow root was good for colds (he blessed me when I sneezed) and the second – given gravely and with pause – was this: 'Remember. You cannot just walk off a mountain.' I had puzzled over its wisdom and meaning but never thought to consider it literally until now, some twenty-six years later.

My wisdom – probably because I had not engaged with map or compass to get us up here – was not listened to now. Purple moor grass, sedges and moss gave way to low heathery mats and dense tangles of bilberry and crowberry. Negotiating such complicated terrain for so long was exhausting. We bickered about whose fault it was to abandon map and compass, and about how much difficulty we were really in – or not. Visibility had become poor and it was now raining hard. But we chivvied and goaded and cheered each other on.

The going became increasingly steep and difficult, and we were thwarted again and again by scree or sheer drops. The mountain began to gather the rainwater to its burns and throw it off outcrops, as if they were gargoyles on a slate church roof. Glimpsed through cloud on the opposite hillside, they looked like static white forks of lightning. As the waterways deepened, so did the chasms we crossed and as the bracken thickened treacherously, our slips became more frequent and more alarming. Yet when we reached at and grasped handfuls of myrtle, it held, releasing its wonderful scent; and when we did fall – and Rosie rolled – the purple heather was soft, yielding and, according to Rosie, 'bouncy as a mattress' and thus ripe for staged, clown-like falls, accompanied by contagious shrieks of laughter.

To the children, this was now a proper adventure that they were stoically trying not to tire of, making up 'marching songs' about being lost on the mountain and what they were looking forward to when they got back. But my husband and I – experienced walkers – were beginning to feel a little irresponsible and foolish. We stopped, reconsidered, drank the last of the hot chocolate and ultimately, scrambled back up on all fours to reach a point where we could angle our descent less steeply. We finally reached the soft hush of pinewood and the road with relief and a humble sense of achievement, not long before dark.

On our last evening, when the sun returned, we cooked tea in the shingle crescent of an ox-bow in the cola-coloured river. Wet otter prints were drying on the stones.

We gazed up at Beinn na Sroine, 'The Offended Mountain', and hoped that it wasn't. A very large bird came over the summit. Heart thumping wildly, I yelped and grabbed my binoculars. 'What's that…? Surely that's…!' Even at three thousand feet up and still struggling with a sense of proportion, there was no doubt: here were the 'flying barn door' proportions of a golden eagle's two-metre wingspan.

Then something extraordinary happened. We were about to get a last lesson in scale. What appeared to be rabbits suddenly poured over the ridge. With astonishment, I realised they were red deer, Britain's largest land mammal, and the eagle was driving them forward.

Nothing could have prepared us for what happened next.

With two pairs of binoculars between the five of us, we watched hinds and calves bound down the mountain, the eagle in leisurely airborne pursuit. The raptor separated the herd and singled out a fleeing calf, sandwiched between two hinds, and swooped on it repeatedly.

We swapped and reswapped the binoculars, hopping up and down when we don't have them, reporting live when we do: 'What's it doing now?' I asked. 'It's chasing them off the mountain!' came the reply. 'Wait, no, the deer are standing up to it!' With the calf losing pace, the herd stopped to face the bird, which hovered momentarily just above the leading deer. I have never seen a deer look skyward before, but on the ridgeline, the two hinds did just that: looked helplessly up at the great, dangling, feathered shanks of the bird. One reared and struck out. The eagle dropped onto the calf, hitting it on the withers. The youngster jinked away and the three scurried into the safety of the trees. The eagle, defied yet defiant, drifted back along the ridge without a single wingbeat, and vanished near the trig point.

The mountain had offered us a second, intense, memorable experience. Eagles have been known to try and cause injury to larger prey beyond their capabilities, in the hope of picking it up later. It is rarely witnessed. We were lucky, but we'd also had all our senses open.

We were better acquainted, the mountain and us. And as a family too. Our shared adventure had involved discovery, peril, wonder, arguments, support, hilarity and absolute awe. The wild landscape and its inhabitants had allowed us a deeper understanding, a richer experience.

Our eldest is on the cusp of independent travel. We're planning to buy him a passport for his eighteenth birthday – the age I was when receiving the Tsuut'ina elder's wisdom. But he already has his own real passport to anywhere – a reason to travel, to meet new neighbours from the doorstep, with gentle inquiry and a willingness to be surprised, eyes and all other senses wide open for the best experience ever. He will travel knowing its full worth, gift and boundless opportunity, with the joy of discovery and learning in his heart.

With nature as his and his sisters' passport, their lives will be all the richer. It makes the difference between being a tourist and an explorer, anywhere.

Nicola Chester lives with her family in the North Wessex Downs and endeavours to spend more time outdoors than in. She is an avid naturalist, nature writer, school librarian and the RSPB's longest-running female columnist. She blogs and tweets about her interactions  with the natural world and runs 'wild writing' workshops for anybody in almost every situation, from museums to woods. She dreams of wilder travel.

Encounters with the Galápagos

Jane Vincent-Havelka

'Oh, Madre Mia! Look at all the bugs!' shrieked our three-year-old daughter Mandy as we turned on the lights in our tiny cabin on the small, flat-bottomed ship. She had picked up the expression from an elderly lady on board, and the dozens of cockroaches were permanent passengers.

It was June 1963, and our Canadian family was heading to Ecuador's Galápagos Islands on the monthly supply ship – at that time the only more-or-less-regular way of reaching the islands. We were eager to explore these 'enchanted islands' before tourism discovered them – and had been warned that this would be 'adventure' travel. Along with returning islanders, the ship carried every sort of freight: live sows and piglets, chickens, a sad-looking horse and a multitude of boxes containing everything from sewing machines to mattresses. Our children, Mandy and eleven-month-old Rory, were already very used to travelling but a voyage over open sea would prove a novel experience.

My husband George and I were relieved to be on board. The humidity of Guayaquil port on the Ecuadorian mainland had been hard on the kids, causing both to suffer from fevers. Added to that, Rory was teething and fretful. Happily, though, thanks to various antibiotics, the children were now on the road to recovery. And the doctor had finally given his approval for our departure.

As we pitched and rolled across the Pacific for four days, Mandy supervised the animals – but without realising that some were also our meals. The upper deck was made into a safe playing area, with tarpaulins tied over the railings, and both children developed a passion for the ripening bananas swinging overhead. They made friends with some island kids, and we mothers socialised while hanging out cloth nappies to dry in the wind.

Land at last! We reached Wreck Bay on San Cristobal, the easternmost island of the famed archipelago, and our fellow passengers disembarked. We were sad to see them go: they had been most helpful with the children and full of information on the islands. There was time for us to pay San Cristobal a short visit, too. The crew swung the children down to the rickety wharf, with Rory in his little backpack chair (a state-of-the-art baby carrier in those days). A bone-rattling truck jolted us up into the highlands. We explored the small village of Progresso, with Mandy going wild with energy as she regained her land legs and Rory surveying the scenery from his father's back.

It was soon time to return to the ship. For days we churned around the archipelago, delivering freight and mail to the other inhabited islands – Santa Cruz, Isabela and Floreana. Along the way, we had the opportunity to visit a few of the many desolate dots of land. We marvelled at their barren shores, black lava reefs washed by Pacific swells, great forests of cactus and, on some, lowering volcanic cones.

When we came ashore at one of the Islas Plazas, curious sea-lion mothers and pups flippered up to sit beside the children. Mandy started singing to them – and several replied with sharp barks. A couple of pups edged nearer to sniff her woollen jersey. We sat quietly, watching the gentle interaction. Suddenly Mandy gave a cry of delight – 'Daddy… dragons!' – as dozens of marine iguanas arrived through the surf and hauled their black bodies on to wet rocks forming the shoreline. Inland, on this same barren island of thorns and cactus, our guide Jacob introduced us to a larger 'dragon'. An astonishing animal with spiky crest and inflatable ruff, this land iguana hissed in rage at being disturbed. Undeterred, Jacob grabbed it by the tail and held it up, the reptile's length matching the kids' height and then some. Rory looked puzzled by this creature, and Mandy kept well away, warily undecided whether it was friend or foe.

Back on San Cristobal we were introduced to our first *galápagos*, the giant land tortoise after which the islands are named. This individual had become used to humans, and the children were offered a chance to ride it – something that clearly would be unthinkable in our modern era of rather more respectful interactions with wildlife. It lumbered off, unperturbed, with Mandy 'aboard' and enthusiastically shouting 'look, he's just the right size for me!' while wishing she had reins to guide it. Rory was a little unsure and needed help to balance atop the giant's shell. Mandy was then introduced to two young tortoises. Delightedly, she fed them bananas, accompanying the offering with stern instructions: 'You must eat your bananas if you want to grow into a giant *galápagos*!'

Our ship continued to wallow through the swells among the islands. On the golden sands of Isabela, local children invited our little pair to play tag. There was just one problem: all the motion of travelling across land and sea meant that Rory was not ready to try walking. So instead they all shouted encouragement as Rory crawled as fast as he could until eventually collapsing into an exhausted nap. Meanwhile Mandy got diverted by a local donkey, imploring it to join the fun by rubbing its nose: 'Wake up, burro, and say hello.'

Our island-hopping continued, with new fun at every landfall and many opportunities to meet delightful, talented people who welcomed us into their homes. Rory's first birthday found us on Floreana, where we visited the Wittmer family, who were among the original settlers of the island, in 1932. Dressed in their best clothes, the four Wittmer grandchildren enthusiastically welcomed Mandy and Rory, inviting them to share some cake; on learning about Rory's special day, it was immediately relabelled as birthday cake. Later that day, landing at Post Office Bay, we hoisted up the children to mail letters in the lonely barrel set up by ancient whaling fleets. Tradition demanded that passing ships call into the Bay to collect its contents and send the mail on its way. Mandy was anxious. 'Are you sure they will reach Canada?' We weren't sure at all but our letters did indeed reach Canada, some six months later.

Rory's birthday evening turned into a special event for both our son and the ship. The first mate lent Rory his cap to wear, giving him a quirky appearance. Having no ingredients for a cake, the cook had baked a special loaf of bread, which I decorated with a candle. Rory was pleased with his simple gifts of a plastic boat and an inflatable *galápagos* swim ring that we had bought in Guayaquil. That night the great volcanic cone on Isabela, thirty miles away, lit the sky with a series of crimson salutes. A unique birthday celebration!

By now, the children were hardened sailors, at home with life on our rusty vessel. They loved each day. For them, the rougher the sea, the bigger the joke. Mandy even accepted the sight of the crew butchering the ship's cow on the deck – and then ate the resulting beef stew for supper. That said, she became distressed and teary at the sight of the horse struggling to swim from the boat to the beach. At every landing, the sailors swung the children ashore or passed them from hand to hand. The islanders also treated us to rides on rowing boats and sailing ships. 'I love messing around in boats!' Mandy exclaimed.

At Academy Bay, we joyfully accepted an invitation to visit the Angermeyers, who had settled on the islands a few years after the Wittmers. Each evening they placed a bowl of warm cooked rice on the patio, then whistled. We watched as marine iguanas swarmed up from the sea to feed. 'Rory, NO!' Mandy screamed. As we delighted in the spectacle, Rory decided to join the animals, crawling over to share their meal. The iguanas were quite unconcerned at the intrusion.

On every island, we wondered at distinctive wildlife, meeting many species of birds and other animals found only in the Galápagos. Among the birdlife were odd-looking pelicans and tropical penguins, flightless cormorants and blue-footed boobies, short-eared owls and Darwin's finches. The shores and waves were dotted with brightly coloured Sally Lightfoot crabs, plus numerous fur seals and sea lions. Finally, in dense bush high on Santa Cruz, we were excited to find our first wild *galápagos*. Some 400 pounds in weight, and perhaps a hundred years old, it calmly peered at us with unwinking beady eyes. Such was its bulk that the children could hardly believe their eyes.

As often happens when travelling with children, our time in the Galápagos wasn't entirely problem-free. Poor Rory got covered by mosquito bites and suffered hugely from the resulting itchiness. Mandy got a hand covered with splinters as she grabbed the side of a wooden staircase descending to a beach; it took us an hour to pick them out, with her shrieking blue murder throughout. But these were minor troubles in the overall joy of our magical adventures.

After five days of island visits, our ship had finished its run and was ready to return to Guayaquil. We, on the other hand, were hugely reluctant to leave this fascinating world… so leapt at an invitation to linger on Santa Cruz. Our hostess, Friedel, had invited us to visit her family in the uplands, there to search for yet more Galápagos tortoises. Five days into our stay with them, we were all set to embark on this exciting excursion when suddenly word came that our permit to visit the islands could not be extended. Accordingly we had to return to the mainland. Mandy was distraught. 'But we won't see the *galápagos*!'

Following a mad early-morning dash through rough seas teeming with sharks' fins, we made landfall on Baltra and joined some drunken government officials for the flight to Guayaquil. How we wished we could have waited for the next boat and the friendly crew that had brought us here. But how lucky we were to visit this remarkable place long before it became well known to tourists. Sadly, the children cannot remember their island adventures. But our early wanderings left a legacy. Both Mandy and Rory have become great travellers themselves, loving adventure and the natural world. That said, both would jump at a chance to go back to the Galápagos.

Jane Vincent-Havelka is a Canadian photographer. In 1963, she and husband George spent over a year travelling throughout South America with their two young children. Their writing and photography continued to take them back to the continent, always as a family. After George's death, Jane's focus changed to Asia, particularly the Himalayas and its people. Their daughter Amanda is following in the family tradition, travelling extensively with her own two children (page 166).

Wild, Wet and Wondrous

Amanda Vincent

'Mama, Puddle and Rainbow can help push.' I suppressed my
worry and turned to the two eager young faces in the back
seat of our truck, one child clutching her beloved penguin and the
other his magical unicorn. 'Right,' I said, 'you'd better hop out so we
can all have a go'. After all, given that we were stuck fast in deep sand
on a wild South African beach, with the tide creeping towards us, we
could use all offers of help. Plus they were a particularly well-travelled
foursome who knew how to cope in a tight spot.

It was just after Christmas 2017 when we found ourselves in
iSimangaliso Wetland Park. A precious jewel of a wilderness along
the Indian Ocean, the park lies just south of the Mozambique border.
Having been carted around the world as a young child following my
parents' work, it was perhaps inevitable that I would do the same with
my two kids. Andaya was eleven and Kian eight, and the three of us
were spending a year on field visits to marine conservation projects. I
was on sabbatical from my university, the kids were out of school, and
we were getting stuck into colleagues' work in a handful of countries,
though generally less literally than here...

Our great friend Jean was leading the expedition (planned so
she and I could explore future collaborations). The kids regarded this
a Very Good Thing because Jean was 'super silly and fun', knew all

about wildlife, and had a new *bakkie* – as pick-up trucks are known in South Africa – that was kitted up for bush adventures. I was excited because, as one of the country's most senior conservationists, Jean had special access to remote regions. So here we were, with extraordinary permission to explore the 220-km-long iSimangaliso beach. And explore it we did, from dawn to midnight each day.

'Hurry up, hurry up,' called Andaya. 'I need to get in the water.' We had left the tiny field station early in the morning, taken the roadway through the dunes to the beach and driven along the trackless sand to a series of immense tide pools. We hauled on our fins, spat in our masks to defog them and nudged the snorkels into place. Andaya was first in and immediately popped up, a huge grin on her face. 'It's like being in an aquarium,' she cried gleefully. Sure enough, protected from the surge of the rocky shore, we were immersed in a clear-water symphony for the senses. My professional training kicked in and I began watching the fantastic fish around us. Soon, though, the kids' many snorkel-muted demands that I 'umm n see dis' led me to defer serious marine biology to another day. It was such fun to watch their excitement. Kian followed one favourite fish for ages, in and out of rocky crevices, both of them bounced around by waves. 'It was blue and black and white. It was an angelfish and was beautiful with lots of lines,' he explained later.

Were it not for the real chill of the water, we might still be in those pools. Eventually, though, the kids' cold little bodies drove us out. They rushed up and down a sandy bank to warm up. Then Kian created an elaborate racetrack in the sand for his new hand-carved wooden truck, acquired at a roadside stand a few days earlier. 'Look Mama, it's carrying searchlights and shovels and fuel canisters.' We decided it was a good thing the truck was so well equipped, given its troubles with deep sand – troubles that turned out to be a harbinger of things to come.

We drove north on the beach toward an unusual rocky headland where Jean wanted to show us a mussel conservation project. She navigated expertly, choosing her speed carefully to keep us moving over the ground steadily, while avoiding the granular 'sugar sand' that could bog us down. Jean needed all her years of experience to pick a path that was low enough on the beach not to disturb the marine turtle nests that dotted the dunes but high enough to avoid the incoming tide. As we crossed many turtle tracks, revealing the females' laborious waddle between sea and dunes, the kids became experts at distinguishing the species. 'There's one from a loggerhead,' cried Kian. 'And this one's a leatherback. See, a line down the middle from the ridge on its shell,' noted Andaya. The kids may have been missing school, but they were certainly getting an education. As for me, tired from many months of managing our travel in India, Chile, Argentina and China, I settled back ever so happily and left all the thinking to Jean while the kilometres slipped by.

We were jolted out of our quiet moods by a sudden wallowing of the bakkie, and our friend muttering to herself, 'Now you've done it, Jean'. In avoiding a turtle nest, Jean had gone slightly too far down the beach and we were caught fast in sugar sand. Moreover, we were a bit too close for comfort to the incoming Indian Ocean. We briefly considered our position but there really wasn't much to decide. As we were the only vehicle permitted on the vast beach, we would have to extricate ourselves, and quickly. That's when Puddle and Rainbow proffered their help and we all hopped out. Unfortunately, our combined efforts to push and push and push (while Jean drove) just didn't do the job.

It was time for more ingenious approaches. We tried shoving, heaving, rocking and rolling. No progress. We had already deflated the tyres to drive on the beach but now let out more air. And yet more. It wasn't enough. We all dug and dug, struggling to free tyres and axles. While good exercise, this achieved little. We improvised some sand mats and tried to drive over them. No use. We brainstormed new plans, we cajoled the bakkie and we begged the sand to let go. Amazingly, we also stayed nice to each other, which was not a given under the circumstances, especially since Puddle and Rainbow kept offering, umm, somewhat random suggestions.

Then Kian had one of his good ideas. 'Sticks!' he shouted, grabbing driftwood and grubbing up remnant bits of decaying roots from the dune fringe. We seized them and laid them in front the tyres. Aha, hope, and none too soon. That tide was closing in. We all ran up the beach with Kian, finding what dead roots and bits of fallen branch we could, and ferrying them back to the truck. Many armloads of 'sticks' later, we had contrived a sort of corduroy road and waited with bated breath for Jean to try her luck. The sticks looked horribly flimsy but held as the tyres rolled over them, finally gaining traction. We three cheered with delight as Jean extracted the bakkie, metre by metre, until it was once more on solid ground and we could relax. We had escaped the sand and the tide – and life was good.

Once we were free, there may have been a moment or two when the release from worry and my delay in feeding them led to a slight fracas between the children, but I will never tell. At any rate, several snacks later, we were all happily sharing our joy and pride in an enterprising self-rescue. Andaya joked that 'Jean was just testing to see whether we are real field biologists who can cope with this sort of challenge'. Our credentials confirmed, we leapt into the bakkie and tackled the sand again, picking our way quickly but even more carefully toward the headland to examine its mussel beds.

Later, back at the field station for supper, I may have overdone the analogy that extracting a bakkie from sugar sand was a metaphor for life. 'Even the best of times can bring difficult moments,' I declared. 'If at first you don't succeed, try, try again.' 'Teamwork is often a key to success.' And a reminder of my perpetual favourite: 'If you have a problem, what's the solution?' I am very determined that the kids grow up to be problem solvers rather than whiners... so their ability to cope that afternoon delighted me. But the day had more in store, and their resilience would again be put to the test.

Nightfall saw our faithful bakkie patrolling the beach while we kept our eyes peeled for turtles. Jean had long led turtle conservation projects at iSimangaliso and we were going to see 'her' turtles lay eggs. She had to navigate the bakkie over the sands again, now in the pitch darkness. So the kids and I threw ourselves into the challenge of spotting a turtle or her tracks. 'Who knew a huge marine turtle could be so tough to spot? It's so so dark and the sea glitters confusingly,' muttered Andaya.

Eventually, out of the gloom came the bulky shape we desperately wanted to see, heading inland. We stopped the bakkie and followed the female loggerhead turtle up the beach very stealthily. 'Keep down, Mama, and don't rush her,' Kian reminded me repeatedly, apparently not trusting my research training. We crouched near the female's nether regions. She was immersed in digging a hole, then another hole, then another hole, all to confuse potential egg predators.

The night was growing colder and we had to stay still but the turtle was taking her own sweet time. 'She's so slow. No wonder she has barnacles on her,' whispered Kian. 'Argh, sand in my mouth and down my jacket,' spat Andaya, as the female put in a bit more effort. Still we lay watching her, cramping up in our immobility. 'I wish she'd get on with it,' exhorted Kian. Then, finally – finally! – our female lined up her cloaca over the hole and squeezed out a few perfect round white eggs, dripping with mucus. 'Just like ping-pong balls,' breathed Andaya in my ear. The rapturous look on my kids' faces was probably matched by my own. We were tired and cold and very sandy but we just didn't care. Then the rains hit.

A thunderstorm on iSimangaliso is wonderful; sheet lightning illuminating the surging ocean, the huge expanse of beach, the fringing sand dunes, the nesting turtle… and the bedraggled quartet of humans staring at her bum. The cold rain didn't just dump down. It bucketed down, soaking us to the core. But the kids grinned on, small bodies shivering, eyes fixed on the next string of ping-pong balls to emerge. If this was another test of our field-biologist chops, we three were going to pass it, dammit.

Kian sighed with relief as our turtle at last began to tamp down the sand over her precious investment, the storm illuminating her actions like a stop-motion video. Kian was nearing the end of even his notable stores of resilience. He wasn't sure whether to hang on to the excitement or give in to his tiredness and cry. Luckily, the female decided it was time to head home to the ocean, pausing occasionally to wayfind amid the confusing lightning flashes. We, too, could finally uncurl, water sheeting off our weary bodies. 'Yep, you are field biologists all right,' Jean confirmed. Andaya slipped her icy hand into mine as I told my two water rats how much I loved their strong hearts…

The bakkie wove back up the beach to the field station, the clock nearing midnight. As they warmed up, the kids found new energy in reliving their glorious day, reminding us again and again about the bakkie rescue 'with all our sticks, Mama'. Finally, Kian (ever the planner) moved on, asking 'What will we do tomorrow?' 'Crumbs, I'm not sure,' I replied. 'It might be a bit hard to top today, don't you think?' 'That's all right. Just as long as we have another adventure,' Andaya answered. And Puddle and Rainbow nodded enthusiastically.

Amanda Vincent is Professor of marine conservation at the University of British Columbia in Canada. She travelled extensively as a child, primarily in South America (see the story by her mother, Jane Vincent-Havelka, on page 160), and spent three years working her way around the world as a young adult. A single mother, she raises her own children as travellers, too. For a year in 2017–2018, the trio looped twice around the globe while Amanda participated in field conservation and policy development.

The Trip to Bunny Island

Suzanne Kamata

I first learned of Ōkunoshima from a Canadian friend's Facebook post. She'd shared photos of herself surrounded by feral rabbits. The islet, just off the coast of Shikoku island and only accessible by ferry, was home to hundreds of these adorable animals. How unusual, I thought. And how cute! Surprisingly, few Japanese people I talked to seemed to know about this place. However, the moment she saw it featured on a TV travel show, my sixteen-year-old daughter Lilia, who is deaf and has cerebral palsy, indicated that she wanted to visit.

'It's really far,' I told her. 'At least three hours by car.'

'We can take the bus,' she signed to me.

Being charmed by the idea of an island full of bunnies, I wanted to visit as much as Lilia did, but I knew it wouldn't be easy. I knew that there was no direct bus from our town in eastern Shikoku to Tadanoumi where we would board the ferry to Ōkunoshima. My daughter uses a wheelchair, making changing buses a bit of a hassle. So when I chanced upon a flyer advertising a one-day bus tour to Ōkunoshima, my heart leapt. I immediately signed us up.

We got up extra early that sunny Sunday and met our tour guide in a gravel car park near the town gym. I had told the tour guide that my daughter was disabled, but that it wasn't a big deal. We climbed into the front seat as the guide greeted us with tea and packaged rice balls.

We gazed at lush green terraced fields, yellow roadside wildflowers and flooded rice paddies. The landscape outside our window might have been lifted from the 1988 animated film *My Neighbour Totoro*. '*Inaka*,' Lilia signed. I agreed that we were deep 'in the countryside'.

I was a little worried that, once we reached the island, my daughter would find the real-life rabbits annoying. I remembered how, on a school trip, she had been bothered by the notoriously aggressive deer in Nara Park on the island of Honshu. One hungry animal had even tried to nibble her notebook. What if the rabbits tried to browse her fingers or mobile phone? But as we rolled along the highway, Lilia reminisced about the rabbit that she and kindergarten classmates had once cared for. When the animal died, the children held a little ceremony while burying it.

As we approached the port, finally catching a glimpse of the sea, the tour guide gave us some final instructions. 'Don't give the rabbits snacks,' she said. Instead, we could buy proper rabbit food at the port. The bus turned down a narrow road flanked by brown-tiled houses, many boasting solar panels. Finally we arrived at a car park next to a small cluster of buildings. Although seemingly in the back of beyond, a long line of people already snaked around the corner from the ferry dock. The tour guide seemed a bit nervous. 'It's a small boat,' she said, 'and they don't accept reservations'. She hurried off to buy our tickets.

Upon return, the tour guide informed us that the passengers were lined up for an earlier ferry. We would be able to board our boat, as intended. Phew! With half an hour before departure, we all got off the bus. Lilia and I entered a small building with a big clock to buy packets of rabbit food.

Upon boarding, most passengers went above deck. We were directed to the lower level, along with several young families with buggies. It was shaded and cool. We stayed to one side as three lines of cars were ushered onto the ferry. Lilia, who has always been far more sociable than me, tried to get me to start a conversation with a blonde foreign woman, husband and three kids. I didn't really feel like talking, so resisted my daughter's entreaties, suggesting that we simply relax, enjoying the wind on our faces and the sight of the waves. Nevertheless, I was intrigued. Given that most Japanese people had never heard of Ōkunoshima, it seemed remarkable that several groups of foreigners – on this ferry alone – were bound for the island.

The crossing took twenty minutes. I half-expected hordes of rabbits to greet us upon disembarking, but it was hot. The first bunnies I spotted were lolling beneath bushes, their energy sapped by high temperatures and humidity. I pointed them out to Lilia. 'There, in this burrow. Under that picnic table.'

The tour guide had arranged for a minibus to transport my daughter and me to the Usagi Lunch Café, where our group would eat. It occurred to me that this was the first Japanese island I had visited that wasn't home to stray cats. 'Are there any predators on this island?' I asked our driver. He thought for a moment. 'Maybe crows.'

We arrived at the restaurant. Here diners with a sense of humour could order pancakes branded with bunnies, white rice moulded into rabbit shapes surrounded by curry, and long-eared rice-filled omelettes. After lunch, we set out to explore. The bunnies were not hard to find. On a grassy lawn, we settled in a shady spot under some trees. Some bunnies were similarly seeking solace from the sun, so we tempted them closer by offering titbits. I was worried that they might bite our fingers, but they were docile and friendly, nibbling only on the food offered. '*Kawaii!*' Lilia said. 'Cute!'

Although the rabbits now live in the wild, they are supposedly descendants of domestic rabbits. The most anodyne story goes that, in 1971, children released eight of the creatures on to the island. As is rabbits' wont, they swiftly proliferated: now some seven hundred call it home.

There is an alternative, more sinister theory as to how the rabbits came to inhabit the island. Unbeknownst to many Japanese, from 1929–45 chemical weapons were manufactured for the Japanese Army on Ōkunoshima. This project was so secret that, during this period, the island was omitted from most maps of Japan. The poisonous substances produced – including mustard gas, tear gas and phosgene – were used more than two thousand times against the Chinese during World War II, killing eighty thousand people. Rabbits were allegedly introduced so that the effectiveness of the gases could be tested. A different take on the leporine history is that the current population is descended from test rabbits released after the chemical-weapon facility was destroyed in 1945 by US Armed Forces.

Whatever the truth about the rabbits' arrival, Japan is no longer secretive about Ōkunoshima's poisonous past. Lilia wanted to visit the island's Poison Gas Museum, which she had also learned about from TV. Having toured both the Hiroshima Peace Museum and the Holocaust Museum in Washington DC, she was familiar with the horrors of war and keen to learn more about history. Saving a bit of rabbit food for later, we made our way to a small building with a red-brick facade. The exhibits – gas-making materials, factory-worker clothing and photos – take up only two rooms, but their impact is strong. It is little wonder that the museum guide 'makes an appeal for everlasting peace'.

Back under the hot afternoon sun, we wandered slowly back toward the port, dispensing rabbit food as we went. Perhaps, I reflected, these *kawaii* bunnies were released here to live freely in atonement for those that had suffered and died. On Ōkunoshima, they are now protected from anything that might kill them. Signs prohibiting roadside feeding keeps the rabbits out of the way of oncoming cars. An island of death and war has become one of life and peace. As we lined up for the ferry to return home, my only regret was that we couldn't stay longer. Then again, now that we knew how to get there, we could always hop back.

Suzanne Kamata's memoir, *Squeaky Wheels: Travels with My Daughter by Train, Plane, Metro, Tuk-tuk and Wheelchair*, was published by Wyatt-MacKenzie Publishing in 2019. She contributed a story to volume 11 of *The Best Women's Travel Writing* (Travelers' Tales, 2017). Suzanne and her family live on the island of Shikoku, Japan, where she is an associate professor at Naruto University of Education.

James's First Night Camping

David Lowen

We thought it best to pitch tent just before the light went altogether. There was a flat enough area of grass with tall, straight trees a few yards behind. The wind was getting up and perhaps the trees would provide some shelter.

'Can I help?' asked ten-year-old James. 'You'll need to. I can't do this on my own,' I replied. 'Anyway if you're going to travel as much as you say you want to, you'll have to do this often, quickly and in more difficult terrain than this.'

Between us, we laid out the tent, its blue cloth darker in the moonless evening. By the time we'd pumped up the black pneumatic frame, it was almost night. James climbed in through the porthole door, and I switched on the torch for light as we rolled out the sleeping bags. We were travelling light: just a couple of coats in case it got even colder. And a stick we'd picked up earlier. By now it was pitch black.

'Should I keep my trainers on?'

'It depends if we have to do a runner in the night.'

'Might we?'

'Probably not. But keep them close by. You never know.'

This was to be James's first night in a tent. Birdwatching and wildlife chasing had, until now, been a daytime occupation with occasional accompanied late-evening walks. But a ten-year-old wants more, so here we were. Now it was time for *real* adventure.

There was a hoot somewhere out to our left, beyond the trees, which were now rustling as the wind picked up.

'Tawny owl', said James.

'I suspect he won't be our only visitor.'

Another hoot: closer.

A rustling among the leaves smothering the ground not far from the tent.

'Snakes?'

'If you are in the wild, you must prepare for everything,' I said sagely. 'This tent has a groundsheet which is part of the structure, not separate. So nothing is going to creep or slither in unless it can climb through the porthole.' Privately, I thought perhaps a snake might climb up towards the entrance hole and, by its weight, force it down and slither in. I checked the flap. Snakes were my private nightmare. I didn't want them to become James's too.

'So a wolf or a fox might be out there?' James's voice now bore witness to trepidation over and above excitement.

'Hardly a wolf but a fox, yes. They're nosey and always on the lookout for food.'

I could see James weighing up the chances of both fox and wolf (and snake) as he put his hand on the stick. There seemed little point in telling him to go to sleep. There was too much to hear and possibly see. The trees were more than rustling now and the wind was bashing the side of the tent.

'Why didn't we bring any food?'

'You've had supper, although there is this,' I said, producing a bar of chocolate from my pocket. I could see James smile in the flickering of the fading torchlight. 'But no crumbs. We don't want ants crawling all over us.'

'Do foxes like chocolate?'

'They eat almost anything.'

'Boys?'

'They have been reported to bite babies in prams – but not eat them. At least, not that I've heard. But they'll certainly check out anything, including you. Now try and settle down.'

The wind was now howling and we could hear the trees creaking. 'Could the tent blow away?' James asked. Does this boy *ever* stop asking questions? I sought to reassure him. 'It's pegged down, and don't forget the sewn-in groundsheet. It would be a strong wind which took the tent away with us in it.' Even so, I wondered if perhaps I should check. I could feel the sensation of lifting as the wind blew under the groundsheet. I thought the pegs would hold. But, in truth, I was hardly an experienced camper – and certainly not a wild camper.

It was at that precise moment that we heard a yowl that wasn't the wind. And another. It had to be a fox. Nearer to us came a thumping sound and a scampering. Rabbit? In fact, nervous rabbit raising the alarm?

The torch flickered once more and gave out. 'Sorry, James, I should have checked the battery.' There was barely a weak glimmer of moonlight by which to see.

From outside, there came the sound of snuffling and more thumping. James wanted to see what it might be. He nudged open the porthole flap and found himself looking straight towards a fox. I heard his intake of breath above the howl of the wind. 'Fox. It's looking at me.' I didn't need to tell him to stay still. 'Sure it's not a wolf,' I teased. 'It could be,' James exclaimed. 'A wolf. A wolf! Wow!'

James pulled the flap shut. As he did, there was a thump on the side of the tent. Perhaps the fox was playing with the tent pegs and guys? The owl hooted again, closer still.

'What about a wildcat? Or puma? They've been seen in Cornwall.'

As if on cue, a shrieking yowl and movement across by the trees. Another shriek. 'Domestic cats,' I said, blithely.

'But…'

Another yowl – but hardly a snarl. Nevertheless…

James was at the porthole again, looking out. 'Aargh, something nearly hit me.' He spun round holding his hair and with a look of surprise. 'I felt it. Was it a bird?'

'More likely a bat at this time of night.'

'Bloodsucking bat?'

'I'm really not sure what sort of bats you'd get round here.'

James carefully laced up the porthole.

It was not a quiet night. I am not sure how much sleep James got. I know I didn't get much. A father stays awake as guardian even if ants, owls, hedgehogs, snakes, bats, cats (though not pumas) and foxes (though not wolves) might not be the fiercest of human predators. It's what dads are for. That and making sure the torch battery is charged.

In a thin tent, on a wild night, it is better to say it is 'guardianship' rather than nerves that keep a father awake. With snuffle and thump, howl and hoot, the night passed.

The morning broke, mild and sunny. The wind had eased.

'Hallooo…?' A male voice I recognised vaguely but sleepily.

'Who is it?', said James blearily. Our final test, after the winds and the animals, was now humans – the animals that scare James's hero, David Attenborough, more than any other.

It was James who lifted the tent flap first.

'Oh, James, it's you. Good morning.'

'Hello, Richard. You're up early.'

'It's my flock,' he said. 'They need tending.' He fingered his clerical collar. 'You must have had a wild old night. That wind!'

'Yes,' said James. 'My first night under canvas – but Dad is with me.'

'I can't think of a better place for a first night than your own back garden,' Richard said, thoughtfully. 'Mind you, there must have been a fox around. I heard his yowl and could hear your pet rabbit thumping in his cage.'

'Yes, Sooty is very brave.'

'And so, James,' said Richard, 'are you'. He departed, in service of his congregation.

'Time to wake Mum and Amy and tell them about the wolf and the pumas?', asked James the Brave.

A former journalist, television producer and executive, **David Lowen** now runs an international media consultancy. He is chair of the board of Leeds Beckett University and chairs UCAS Council, responsible for the management of university applications. David is an Honorary Fellow of Emmanuel College, Cambridge, and a Fellow and trustee of the Royal Television Society. He has written two books: one on survival in the wild for children and another on self-defence for women.

THE ROAD TO ENLIGHTENMENT

Travels with My Teen: Edinburgh

Theresa Sainsbury

Edinburgh didn't start well. The new, automatic security gates at London Heathrow airport failed to recognise me. While fourteen-year-old Jamie went straight through with his headphones on, all hi-tech, digital-age swagger, I got a terse instruction – 'Stand to one side, madam' – as the metal barrier refused to budge. Jamie didn't even realise that I wasn't following him, and when I finally boarded the plane five minutes after it should have left – my breathless arrival eliciting a swathe of tuts, sighs and angry expressions from the other passengers – he tried to unravel the problem with his usual dose of brutal humour.

'Perhaps you look the same as someone else?... Or you've just got weak features?... Or maybe you've aged drastically since your passport photo was taken and the machine can't believe it's you? I mean AI is getting pretty clever, but it probably can't second-guess the menopause...'

We agreed on silence till we got there.

We were staying in Jamie's favourite hotel chain, Premier Inn – one step down from a Holiday Inn, a nudge up from a Travelodge – with all the corporate bleakness and lack of personality that teenagers seem to love: reliable Wi-Fi; ice-cream-dispensing machine in reception; temperatures conducive to T-shirts inside whatever the weather outside; and the all-you-can-eat breakfast. And although such hotels originally had the bonus of being cheap, they aren't even that anymore, particularly in central Edinburgh in festival season.

But at least Jamie was happy. 'Happy child, happy parent,' I reminded myself. And once he'd rearranged the room by shoving his bed against the window so he was as far away from me as possible, and sorted out the Wi-Fi code, I barely heard a word out of him other than, 'Can't wait for the breakfast,' as I snapped out the lights. We live ten doors down from a Premier Inn at home; he could have their flaming breakfast every Saturday morning if he wanted for eight quid rather than the couple of hundred or so I've invested in this trip. Was it worth it, I asked myself?

Well, even for the breakfast alone, it was. Jamie ate at least three full meals, making three separate trips to the counter, each plate layered high with fried food and grease.

'Won't need lunch, Mum,' he said. 'You've got to admit, I'm great VFM.' The days Jamie spoke almost entirely in acronyms or some other code. I grasped about half of it. Probably best that way.

Visiting the Edinburgh Fringe was a long-held dream. A holiday that a cranky teen and his middle-aged mum could both enjoy. Or so I'd thought. I'd fantasised about us trekking up Arthur's Seat, climbing the steps to Scott's monument, drinking coffee in a quirky café on Princes Street before taking in a few comedy shows – events for which I'd managed to secure two seats for the price of one, the Fringe equivalent of preview tickets.

But as we returned to our room after the mountainous breakfast, Jamie informed me very firmly that he didn't like climbing mountains anymore after I'd forced him up Snowdon in a gale, that looking at old buildings was for old people, and that all he really wanted to find was the nearest Costa so he could get an iced mocha and catch up with his mates on his phone.

After the mocha (cortado for me), we spent the afternoon wandering, taking in the architecture. Or, at least, I gave it a try. Once we'd done the Royal Mile (lovely views), Jamie all crotchety and dragging his feet, I swiftly gave up and switched to the lure of Princes Street with its retail therapy. We were here for the comedy, I had to remind myself, so perhaps I should stop trying to force my other interests on him.

'Let's split up for a while,' I suggested.

'Just checking where the nearest Foot Asylum is,' he said, huddled over his phone. 'Might need you for your student discount.'

I had this awful feeling that Foot Asylum was the store with headache-inducing lighting and pounding house music, the one where he spent ages flicking through rails of synthetic clothing, trying on oversize trainers. I was definitely being persecuted: even my brave decision to go back to 'school' and study for a Masters course had snookered me. After half an hour of retail hell, I escaped to Jenner's department store, an architectural gem in itself, for a grown-up cup of Earl Grey tea.

At 6.30 p.m. Jamie and I regrouped, me feeling cautiously optimistic about our first show. I strode ahead.

'Mum,' he yelled.

I turned around. He was staring at his phone yet again.

'We're going the wrong way,' he said, without lifting his head. A statement delivered with all the confidence of a teenager who understands exactly how to manipulate a smart phone. Unlike me.

I moved closer, looked at Jamie's version of Google Maps. The tiny diagram on his phone wasn't moving around like mine, circling as I circled, sending my already sketchy knowledge of left and right to somewhere even more vague and hazy.

'Why is your map staying still?' I demanded.

A deep sigh followed by a dismissive response. 'Get yourself a copy of the instruction manual.' It was muttered, barely audible, but I caught it.

'I've switched off screen rotation,' he said very slowly, deciding to humour his technologically illiterate mother. 'Anyway, it's a left, then a right, then a long walk down a straight road. Takes fifteen minutes.'

'You lead,' I said, by way of thanks, 'as you seem to be good at this'.

'As you *should* be. Haven't you got a geography degree?'

'Yes – but we read paper maps in my day.'

'Ahh, no *buts*, Mum. To quote one of your favourite sayings when *I'm* trying to wriggle out of something.'

I shook my head. He was far too sharp. I was tempted to go down the 'don't-be-cheeky' route but pulled back. We were on holiday after all.

We started walking again, Jamie in front and me behind, moving with the crowd, not against it, as we had been all afternoon. It felt good to be in someone else's slipstream.

The nearer we got, the more my cautious optimism ebbed. I started overthinking the comedy act that I'd booked for our first evening, panicking that despite all my careful research, it would fail to hold any appeal for Jamie. Until now, I had kept up a steady stream of positivity, a line of non-confrontational drivel that all us middle-class, liberal 'I'm-too-scared-to-fall-out-with-you' parents are so good at. But now, the doubts were creeping in on all fronts.

The show didn't start until 7.30 p.m., and we couldn't be more than ten minutes away. That meant a potentially long wait in a queue. There is always a queue at the Fringe, because seats are not allocated. Moreover, the lines tended to be lengthy and good natured, with well-spoken, lanyard-wearing attendants keeping the human column tidy and trotting out precisely the kind of chatty claptrap that my teenage son finds so offensive. Perhaps he could just keep himself plugged in? Yes, I'll suggest that.

'We must be close,' I said. There were well-intentioned lanyard-wearers everywhere.

'Who are you seeing?' called one.

'Pete Firman,' I replied.

'Straight on and the queue is directly in front of you.'

'I've never heard of Pete Firman,' Jamie said. 'Is he any good?'

'Magic plus comedy. The bit I watched on YouTube looked promising.'

'I quite like magic,' he mumbled.

The queue was of medium length, youngish, but with a notable absence of kids. I pulled the tickets out of my bag and ran my finger over the stipulation '**14+ only**' written in bold at the bottom. I kept my finger in place and nudged Jamie. A smile. He didn't like small children who ran around shouting, their hapless parents having lost all sense of control. Ironic that he and I were like that until about two years ago. I still hadn't managed the control bit, but at least he'd started caring about what other people thought of him.

The queue started moving fifteen minutes before showtime. I didn't want to jinx it, but things were looking up.

The theatre was small, and the teen and I were placed seven rows back, in the centre. Bang on time, Pete Firman took to the stage, and the next fifty-five minutes passed at breakneck speed. Jamie laughed, squeezed my arm at tense moments, clapped endlessly. I heard numerous sharp intakes of breath. Pete Firman was a rip-roaring success. No, more than that, he'd saved my summer holiday.

'No encore,' I whispered as Jamie remained standing at the end. 'They need to get ready for the next performer.' We joined the line filing out.

'Ten out of ten,' Jamie said, unprompted. I stared at him, snatching the olive branch he was offering. I almost floated back to the hotel.

Jamie lay on his bed as I read my Kindle. Holding his phone at arm's length, no headphones this time, he was watching old clips of Pete Firman. He was laughing his *Blackadder* laugh, the one that meant he was finding it properly funny.

'Firman's doing panto near us at Christmas,' Jamie asked. 'Shall I book seats?'

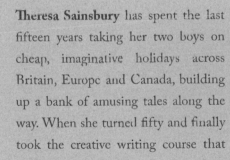

Theresa Sainsbury has spent the last fifteen years taking her two boys on cheap, imaginative holidays across Britain, Europe and Canada, building up a bank of amusing tales along the way. When she turned fifty and finally took the creative writing course that she'd be thinking about for years, the stories had the courage to emerge. When not writing and travelling, Theresa teaches GCSE English to teenagers.

Looking Up

Dom Tulett

I remember the tram. I remember its colour, its shape, its passengers. I remember its serene approach, gliding smoothly on rails that glinted with springtime sun, rolling through a stop, moving up the road, passing the men selling grilled sweetcorn under the watchful gaze of the Hagia Sophia. We were sat on a bench in the cool Istanbul air, greedily gnawing away at our snack, spilling as many little yellow cubes as we ate, Heidi swinging her legs in opposite, absent-minded rhythm beneath her. And I did what I always do – I pictured my daughter jumping down from her seat, rushing out across the road, and I pictured the tram screaming a dirge of angry metal brakes, raging against the inflexible will of physics, spitting sparks and bracing time. Though she showed no signs of leaving her seat, I instinctively shuffled closer to Heidi, placed a hand on her knee and said: 'Careful'.

Before Heidi arrived, every spare pound and every spare day went towards travelling. My wife and I made sure we would take one substantial trip each year – East Africa, Latin America, the Indian subcontinent – with as many short stops and weekend breaks as possible stretching the ranges of the calendar. When we decided to start a family, we hoped that lifestyle would continue, but the girl we brought into the world came without a functioning sense of danger, and with an endless supply of energy as a wicked compensation.

It is impossible to tell how many times I directed the word 'careful' to Heidi in the first three-and-a-bit years of her life, each time accompanied with a fearful wince as she climbed or ran or grabbed or wandered, not perceiving the macabre near-future I saw. For our own sanity, and to minimise the risks, we sought out reasons to not travel: the flights will be too difficult; Heidi might not like the food; a bad experience will put us off travel forever. Really we knew that we just might not handle the pace; it would simply be too hard. So we hid her from the world, our precious thing. But really we hid the world from her. We had a colourful map on the wall of her room, and would read bedtime stories of far-off lands, recounting the trips her mother and I had taken as younger adults, but all these tales simply served as forbidden inspiration.

The urgent, remorseless peer pressure of social media shook us out of our discomfort zone. Envious of a couple of friends who had taken advantage of parental leave to travel with their two children to Asia for a month, we resolved to take a trip ourselves, even if not quite so far afield. We battled through another day of Heidi's relentless questions, perpetual motion and blind risk-taking and, collapsing on the couch after we had wrangled her into bed, identified a clear weekend.

'So, where shall we go?'

'Somewhere on the train, no more than a couple of hours from here.'

'OK.'

Bottle, glasses, corkscrew.

'By the sea maybe?'

'OK, yes. Brighton? Or Broadstairs?'

Pour, drink, repeat.

'Could we manage France?'

'On the Eurostar? I don't know. What do you think?'

Within an hour, we had tickets in the inbox for a long weekend in Istanbul.

The flight out there was hard – as difficult as we had imagined. Heidi refused to sit still through the early-morning departure, fiddling with the tray table and kicking the seat in front of her, raging when it was time to clip in her seat belt. Snacks and games and her favourite cartoons on the tablet failed to sooth or distract. The cabin crew brought crayons, paper, stickers and sympathy; other passengers were not so generous. I was those passengers once – I couldn't blame them.

Heidi chatted ceaselessly on the train from the airport to the city – questions that could not be answered, an internal monologue that had broken free. 'Why has that man got a beard? Daddy, I can see a flag. That girl has pink shoes. When does this train stop?' I couldn't match Heidi's energy and struggled to find suitable responses, my brain defeated by the early start and emotionally draining flight.

The receptionist at our hotel – a modern place wedged into the ancient bustle of the central Sultanahmet district – welcomed us with a pocket map that folded out across the expanse of his desk and he marked it up with a flurry of circles, arrows and lines. His final recommendations were closer to home: 'The spa is in the basement. The restaurant is on the ground floor. You can go to the roof to see the views.'

At first we felt that less was more, that staying close to the hotel would enable us to have a simpler trip, so we started our Istanbul break at the bottom – the water was cold and there were no lifeguards, but a swimming pool was familiar territory, something we could handle. Afterwards, we had dinner in the hotel's restaurant, then hurried Heidi to an early bedtime ('Which room is ours? Why is the carpet blue? Can I have two stories? I want to go to the roof.'). Before switching out the light, I asked Heidi what she thought of Istanbul.

'I don't know,' she said. It was her standard response to many questions, but this time I felt that she meant it. She had seen glimpses of the city through the windows of the train, but little else.

The next day, we finally poked our heads out of the comfort blanket of the hotel and ambled down to the Bosporus. Heidi was initially captivated simply by watching the water, but it didn't slow her down for long. I clasped her hand tightly, convinced that she would somehow fall into the river or wander into the road. She buzzed around the streets, dragging us to keep up her pace, entranced by everything she saw, asking questions, squealing whenever we passed a café and she saw the glistening trays of sugared sweets shining in the window displays. 'Mummy, sweets! I know how to count to fourteen - a-million. Has my friend Daniel been to Turkey? I need a wee.' Her energy outlasted ours, even without the sugar rush she so desperately craved.

We ate sweetcorn in Sultanahmet Square and wandered around the dusty lanes near the Grand Bazaar, then hurried along dark, covered alleyways where men sat on small metal chairs at small metal tables, sipping steaming glasses of rich, black coffee. But all I really saw were the trams, the dogs, the potholes in the pavements. 'Careful,' I fretted, again and again, my hand gripping tighter each time.

As the day closed, we collapsed back into the hotel lobby's armchairs. Heidi's energy had still not dipped. 'I have an itch in my wellies. Is tomorrow the next day? I want a chocolate cake for my birthday. Please can I go to the roof?'

'OK,' I replied. 'Just five minutes.'

We let the elevator carry us to the top floor and stepped out into the night sky. The rooftop was deserted and dark. My wife and I scanned the area for danger – low walls, trip hazards, anything sharp – but we needn't have bothered. Heidi looked out across the city, a skyline of a dozen centuries, and for the first time was silent and still. Then she changed her view, craned her neck and looked up. The skies of Europe and Asia met, sewn together in a patchwork of galaxies. Her hand relaxed in mine, for once not straining for release. I let her go, but she stayed close. She spoke again: 'Stars!'

I followed her in looking up. 'Yes, they're beautiful, aren't they?'

She didn't cut her gaze or turn to me, just stared straight up at the universe. 'I've never seen actual twinkly stars before.'

I hated myself that my daughter had passed three without seeing real stars and imagined what other wonders I had withheld from her. I tried to console myself that back home there's more light pollution and it's normally cloudy and we make sure she goes to bed at a sensible time, but still, she'd made her point – I realised that we had spent too much time looking down, too fearful of imagined lows to experience actual highs.

The next day, we resolved to look up. We went back to the waterfront and sat hypnotised as gulls swooped above the cars streaming off the ferries, shipped across from Asia. We watched men fishing off the Galata Bridge, their rods all positioned at the same upward angle, like the necks of a herd of giraffes. We strolled around the Hagia Sophia and the Blue Mosque, and this time we looked up to the skies and the spires, and we noticed the pale pink blossoms of the trees in the park. I gave Heidi some space, loosened the reins, relaxed.

Travelling with Heidi was hard. But a trip to the park's hard, bedtime's hard, getting her to eat green vegetables is hard. Travelling's no harder than all that really, and its rewards are so great. Seeing a cityscape of centuries-old buildings stacking up away from the water, with minarets dominating the skyline; hearing the wailing calls to prayer reach out across the rooftops; breathing in the sweet smell of pastries as we passed the hundreds of cafés that dotted the city;

marvelling at the countless pastel shades of Turkish delight. All of this was surely far more interesting and exciting for a three-year-old than the same grey houses we pass, under the same grey skies, on the same grey way to nursery, day after day after day. Children don't even need to see the tourist-grabbing sites — adults don't either — it's the daily differences that amaze, and they're frequently much more accessible.

On the flight home, Heidi sat in quiet acceptance of her surroundings, the questions and comments silenced temporarily. I like to think that the short taste of the wider world helped her, calmed her, enlightened her, and that our increased trust in her did the same. I also like to think that since that trip, Heidi has thought back to seeing the ferries cross between continents, to wandering the spice-fumed cobbles of history's streets, to beaming with delight as the corn-seller called her a princess; that she's remembered all that and would like more of it. The early signs were good. As the plane banked over the city and we pointed out to her the Hagia Sophia and the Blue Mosque and the wide sweep of the Bosporus down below, Heidi pressed her face against the glass, taking it all in — the right kind of looking down.

Dom Tulett lives with his family in Harpenden, UK. On his daily commute to London he writes stories for his children about the places to which he's travelled. Alongside these, he has recently finished writing a novel set during the final months of the civil war in Sri Lanka. In 2017, he won Bradt Travel Guides' New Travel Writer of the Year award.

Travelling, Differently

Penny Wincer

On a chilly April morning in west Wales, seven-year-old Arthur scuttled ahead of me down the winding country road. I didn't mind that he was right in the middle of the lane. With high hedges on either side and the long stretch of tarmac ahead of us, the central strip was probably the safest and most visible spot. Besides, I didn't want to break the magic. The cold had forced me to rug up in woolly jumper, coat and walking boots, yet Arthur skipped lightly on his toes, barefoot and clad only in pyjamas.

My son had already discarded his jacket, now being cradled in my arms. His signature toe-walking, common in autistic kids such as Arthur, made him appear to glide over the stone-strewn road. As we made our way downhill, we passed another walker, who smiled at Arthur's partial attire and clear excitement at the beach that was cleaving into view. Arthur started to run, flapping his arms wildly, laughing as the crashing waves of Penbryn became visible. I raised my pace to keep up.

A distant figure and a dog were the only living creatures on the beach. The sky was steel-grey but clear of rain. In other, more accessible parts of Britain, such a large expanse of sand probably would have been filled with early-morning ramblers and dog walkers. But not at Penbryn. Here Arthur could run, spinning his arms like a pinwheel, could jump up and down with exhilaration at the crashing tumble of breaking waves, and could toss handfuls of sand into the air then watch them drift downwards. Here Arthur had complete freedom to follow his instincts without the constraints of propriety to hold him back. It was for this liberation – this *release* – that we had driven six long hours the previous day.

I had stopped travelling with Arthur since his difficulties became apparent when he was about two years old. Days out were hard enough given Arthur's frequent meltdowns, severe eating restrictions and inability to engage in activities that other children usually enjoyed. So it seemed just too painful for everyone involved to throw into the mix overnight stays. We were broke anyway, I told myself, with freelance careers barely covering the costs of two young children and private therapies. So why waste money on something that might lead to a nervous breakdown?

This was a profound shift in approach from the frequent international travel that had characterised my work as a photographer, not to mention a childhood spent partly on the hoof, trailing after my similarly freelance and itinerant father. When starting a family, I had envisioned family gap years, frequent trips back to Australia and children well versed in both airport etiquette and foreign food. It had simply never occurred to me that I might end up with a child who would find travel – with its inherent uncertainty, its need for flexibility and curiosity – so intensely difficult as to render it impossible for many years.

The year that Arthur turned five and my daughter Agnes three was also the year that I became a single parent. Determined not to drown in a sea of self-pity, I became fixated on getting us away for the first time in years. A very kind client offered up his beautiful Georgian home in the seaside town of Deal – just a short drive from our London home.

With an awful lot of chips, ice creams (for the kids) and gin (for me), we made it through our inaugural holiday as a family of three. It was far from easy, of course. A crowded beach proved a tricky place to look after Arthur, as he frequently dashed out of sight, caught up in his own world and not being verbal enough to say his own name. Many were the heart-stopping moments when I feared that I had lost him. Although slightly broken and exhausted, we were nevertheless alive – and determined to holiday again.

The beach, or any combination of sand and water, proved such a mesmeric pull for Arthur that it seemed logical to make them the focus of our subsequent trips. Unfortunately, beach houses are expensive ways to holiday – and all the more so for a single parent with an erratic income. Accordingly, over the next couple of years, I selected cheap and remote spots in which to tentatively expand our family travels. This led to the happy discovery that domes, cabins and converted buses are just about the most fun places to stay with small kids, especially noisy ones who lack the social skills to sit nicely at a restaurant or resist digging their hands into pristine flower beds.

It was on a work trip to Wales that I discovered the wonderful hideaway of fforest, near Cardigan. Large domes with wood burners, traditional Welsh blankets, sheepskins and a large clear plastic window through which to watch the inevitable rain come down. After a shaky start the first evening – an anxiety-induced meltdown about sleeping in a bed other than his own – Arthur woke with a huge smile, demanding to go immediately to the beach. I threw on my clothes, sent Agnes to play with friends who were renting an adjacent dome, then followed Arthur as he strode off, shouting for me to follow him down the lane.

Once on the beach, Arthur was tearing off his pyjamas, deeming surplus to requirements even that thin layer of clothing. I laughed, huddling inside my coat from the strong wind, as underpant-clad Arthur happily braced himself and squealed with joy as fine sand was whipped out in arcs from his extended hands. It took perhaps an hour for Arthur to shiver. He came over to me for 'clothes on', lower lip shaking. I helped my son dress, bundling him up in a woolly hat and extra jumper, and suggested that it was time for breakfast.

During the next few days of walks down to the beach and fireside evenings, Arthur relaxed into the trip. In the fields, and on wide and deserted beaches, he was free from my nagging and cajoling, untethered from the demands put on him in our day-to-day life. At school he spends huge amounts of energy on sitting still, completing tasks without distraction and listening to verbal instructions, all things that he finds extremely difficult. Here, on a remote Welsh beach, Arthur was free to be himself.

Since that trip we have enjoyed many more travels. More cabins, outdoor fires and compost loos. A converted bus with snuggly bunk beds, complete with curtains, from which Arthur refused to budge. A group camping trip in which Arthur spent the entire weekend in just his pants, covered in mud, playing happily while the other children ran through woodland, building dens and making up games.

Now it's with glee that Arthur repeats 'holiday!' as I prepare him for a trip. Not even the first night away makes him anxious. Instead he falls into the pattern that we now follow when arriving at new places, including testing out all the beds and getting cosy underneath blankets, with a favourite show on the iPad to bring a familiar element to the new space.

Our travel is not yet unrestrained. Arthur is yet to journey abroad or by plane. With their multiple transitions and ability to turn queuing into a sport, airports are somewhat beyond what we can cope with presently. But with car travel becoming a little easier, I can foresee ferry trips followed by long drives into Italy. In the meantime we have the whole island of Britain to discover. There are so many beaches and lakes to visit, camper vans to try out and forests in which to pitch tents. As long as there is seclusion and some water to play with, it's on my list to try.

This might be a far cry from a year of world-schooling in southeast Asia, which was the kind of family adventure I once envisaged. But in this family we have learnt to focus on all that we have, not what we lack. The possibilities, although not endless, are still vast.

Melbourne-born **Penny Wincer** is a freelance interiors and lifestyle photographer. She lives in south London with her two children, one of whom is autistic. She writes about learning to embrace neurodiverse family life, as her son Arthur teaches her to see the world a little differently.

Thomas and the Great Japanese Farewell

Marie Kreft

'Wow, look at those big mountains!' Vincent pressed his nose and fingertips to the coach window. At four years old he was often fishing for 'wows'. But the Japanese mountain range held my gaze too, with mist-swirled peaks rising from dense, dark woodland. I think this was Aokigahara, the Sea of Trees. Asian black bears inhabit its coniferous depths, perhaps *yurei* too: restless spirits.

'They look so mysterious. We must be nearly there now,' I told him. 'Are you excited?'

'Yeah! I hope we see Thomas and James and Percy and Gordon and Emily...'

Half listening to Vincent's chatter, I watched my son become enchanted by the unfamiliar landscape and hoped today would be a 'wow' day. It felt big, leaving the rest of our family sixty miles away in Tokyo and travelling – just the two of us – to the foot of Mount Fuji. Vincent's brother was only six months old and I missed him already. But I knew my husband and baby would be happy together, pram-wheeling through the gleaming malls of Shinjuku. For Vincent and me, the fleeting nature of childhood and the now-or-never spirit of travel had presented us with a day that needed seizing.

Since Vincent's second birthday, our life had been split between reality and the fictional world of Thomas the Tank Engine. Railway tracks could be found in paving stones, the TV remote was called the Fat Controller, and wooden railway scenes sprung up daily across our living-room rug, populated by runaway cows and tumbling bridges.

Vincent was Thomas-crazy, his love deepened by our good fortune in living close to Thomas Land at Drayton Manor, a theme park in Staffordshire. Over the past two summers Vincent and I had spent many Fridays riding round and round in Lady's Carousel then up and down in Harold the Helicopter. Aged two, Vincent had thought the engines were alive; as he grew wiser we'd invent stories about them coming alive. The piped sweetshop scent, the looped Thomas songs, the always-surprising whoosh of Cranky the Crane's drop tower: these memories are now inextricably linked, for me, with the joy of Vincent's early childhood.

But here was August again and, when its languorous days gave way to September, Vincent would start school. Already I'd seen signs that his passion for Thomas was dwindling, making way for Star Wars and superheroes. So when planning our trip to Tokyo, I put Fuji-Q Highland at the top of my wish list. The amusement park is home to the world's only other Thomas Land, and I hoped a last hurrah with Thomas there would provide a happy ending to this sweet chapter in our lives.

The day was overcast – nearly dull enough to suppress the drama of Fuji-Q's setting near Japan's famous volcanic mountain. Looking out from the coach at the ascents and plummets of the fierce Fujiyama, once the world's tallest rollercoaster, I wished I could view Mount Fuji from the ride's 79-metre peak. The child-free me would have screamed to go faster. But travel was so different now I was a parent: fewer thrills and many more spills, I decided, watching Vincent drop a bag of trail mix over his legs. 'This is Great Cran!' he declared, retrieving an oversized dried cranberry from the crack between our seats. I giggled. We were the only people on the coach who were making any noise.

We missed our stop, winding up lost in a hotel forecourt and wasting valuable Thomas time while I figured out how to get us back. Eventually joining the shuttle train bound for Fuji-Q, standing-room only, Vincent bounced around excitedly, occasionally forgetting to hold on. '*Kawaii!*' young Tokyoites exclaimined at the sight of him. Cute. I wondered how I'd ended up in charge of a child, so trusting and entirely forgiving of my mistake, halfway across the planet.

Fuji-Q's Thomas Land was laid out differently to its Drayton Manor counterpart yet felt strangely familiar – a theme-park British town transposed to east Asia. A dreamworld where you know instinctively where you are but not how to reach anything you need. Families milled around Mrs Kyndley's Kitchen and Lady Topham Hatt's Pavilion. Balloons and carousel music and the smell of katsu curry drifted through the air, which was cooler than in Tokyo but still more cloying than that of any English summer day. The humidity clumped my hair, left Vincent's cheeks flushed.

We started out in a circus-styled maze, constructed from giant wooden crates. Inside it felt confining and the exact opposite of fun, with the only link to Thomas pressed into engine-shaped ink stamps that guests were encouraged to collect. Hot and lost, and fed up with being nudged by similarly hot, lost people, I cheered when Vincent asked whether we could try something else.

We borrowed pairs of Crocs-style shoes, rented two plastic sleds and spent a noisy half-hour hurtling down a pile of artificial snow, occasionally blasted by a ride attendant with a snow machine.

The only link to Thomas was in pictures on the colourful hoardings surrounding us, but Vincent didn't notice. He shrieked with laughter, and I hushed my inner eco-worrier, she who frets about the environmental cost of maintaining snow in summer. We played until the ice numbed our toes.

Not wishing to miss out on rides, we grabbed food on the run: hot dogs and orange juice; Thomas-shaped pancakes; ice cream and snacks of delicious deep-fried 'hurricane' potatoes, twizzled around sticks. We climbed aboard Everybody Twist, a carousel featuring small versions of popular engines. We got Bill, or maybe Ben. The ride played a jangly Thomas theme as it whirled us around, and people sang along while clashing the tambourine that had been hooked over their train's funnel. Vincent looked confused and mildly embarrassed as I joined in as best a cynical Brit can. Then he asked if we could go again.

Our day took a downward turn on Thomas and Percy's Fun Ride: a story journey in miniature trains, narrated in Japanese via loudspeakers and featuring popular characters from the TV series. It was funny until the unexpected appearance of Diesel 10, a devious engine, flexing his dreaded hydraulic roof-top claw. I heard Vincent take a deep breath and felt his small, clammy hand grab my own. It got worse. As we rounded a bend, Vincent caught sight of a scene from which he'd always cowered: Henry the green mainline engine bricked into a tunnel.

'MUMMY!' he hissed, tightening his grip on my hand. 'I never, ever want to go on this again.'

I understood: the Henry episode had upset me as a child too. But to my frustration Vincent was now spooked and refused to board anything else Thomas-related.

'Look – those children are all younger than you and they're not frightened,' I told him, tugging his hand to lead him to a gentle train ride.

'But the Troublesome Trucks have horrible faces,' he said, digging his sandals into the platform. 'I'm. Not. Going!'

At times like this a mother-logue runs through my head: a combination of things my parents said to me, and annoying sayings all of my own. Occasionally I can silence it, but often it bursts out. 'You don't realise how lucky you are!' I started to shout. Vincent had no idea what it meant for our family to be in Japan, to have this experience.

But of course he had no idea. Vincent was four. The world was still so achingly new to him. Steve and I had dragged him across it to fulfil our own neon dreams of Tokyo and prove to ourselves that children are no barrier to travel. And to set the tone for the childhood we longed to give our sons. adventure-filled and happy.

'Come on, sweetheart.' I coaxed Vincent into the Thomas Land theatre. Although the film was in Japanese and incomprehensible to my monoglot brain, I felt confident that it would follow a plot similar to many other Thomas stories: engine causes confusion and delay; engine is bumped, decommissioned or bricked up in a tunnel; engine learns its lesson and vows to be Really Useful next time.

Cooling down in the air-conditioned auditorium, I felt glad when Vincent snuggled into me, chuckling at Thomas's capers watched through oversized 3D glasses. He was content again, and I vowed to be a Really Useful Mother for the rest of the day.

'There's time for one more ride,' I told him. 'What do you think we should choose?'

With a moment's thought, Vincent requested a 'blue rollercoaster' he'd spotted from afar. The Great Fluffy Sky Adventure featured cute hamster characters but, as we wove past popcorn stands and sky bicycles to reach its entrance, I realised that this ride was going to be higher, faster and scarier than anything in Thomas Land. You couldn't make this boy up, my husband Steve would say.

'Are you sure?'

Vincent nodded with such vigour that his head looked in danger of falling off. The ride attendant, a teenage boy, stilled it gently by moving Vincent towards a vertical measuring chart and crowning him with a smooth wooden plank.

'OK, tall enough,' he said. 'You can go.'

'Yes!' Vincent leapt into the queue, through which we would shuffle for almost two hours. I felt hungry, hot and footsore but Vincent's energy was unending – his commentary about the park, the people and the ride earning coy smiles from young couples.

Our reward for queuing was two minutes spent hurtling through the air in a car shaped like a cloud flown by hamsters: Vincent in front, me behind. He yelled into the wind with such blissful abandon that I almost ignored the rushing sensation of the rollercoaster and simply watched him, his hair blown back, grin broad.

On the way back to our coach, Vincent was keen for my opinion.

'Were you really, really scared, Mummy?'

'Ooh, a little bit, yes. But I loved it too. How about you?'

'Nope. I wasn't scared at all. It was the best ride in the world!'

During a spell of quiet darkness between the dusky highway and Tokyo's Friday-night lights, Vincent fell asleep in my arms. I put my hand in his damp and tousled hair. This was the best ride in the world, I thought: having children, helping them grow. I couldn't wait to see Steve and, as I was still breastfeeding, ached to be back with baby Alexei. But I'd had the most precious day with my firstborn. Now I resolved to stop feeling sad about the Thomas pyjamas that were becoming too small; the once-beloved wooden engines that were increasingly losing out to lightsabres. Bring on the 'wows' of rollercoasters and mysterious mountains, I decided. Vincent's toddlerhood was now in the past, but the biggest and best fun of his childhood stretched out like railway tracks ahead.

Marie Kreft is a former winner of the Bradt Travel Guides/*Independent on Sunday* travel-writing competition. She is the author of *Slow Travel: Shropshire* for Bradt and has been published in several national titles, including *BBC Countryfile* magazine. Marie and her now husband Steve Wilkes have backpacked halfway across the world together; now they're trying to instil their love of adventure in their two young sons. They live in Birmingham, UK.

How to Lose Weight
on Vacation

Jen Dowd

I've never been able to follow the traditional weight-loss-on-the-road advice, and honestly, who would want to? Eat a healthy breakfast. Don't snack. Walk more. Take the stairs. Self-cater. No thank you. Trying all the food and wine and beer and coffee is one of the best parts of being on vacation. No consequences. No rules. Just carbs.

The national food of Georgia, where our family of four recently vacationed, is *khachapuri*, a traditional cheese-filled bread dish eaten at any and all meals. Beer costs less than a dollar in Tbilisi. And no dinner is complete with a plate of *khinkali*, delicate Georgian dumplings filled with spiced pork, herbs and garlic. Moderation is clearly not the name of the game for anyone sitting down to enjoy a Georgian meal.

But don't worry, fellow chocolate-and-wine-lovers, do I have a solution for you! Abandon your healthy eating efforts and measly attempts at exercise and just take two small children with you on your travels instead – I promise, you'll never finish a meal again.

In their defence, our children usually eat breakfast like champs. It's perfect kid-meal material – eggs, fruit, bread, maybe some juice. At breakfast they're rested, cheerful and excited about the day.

Then there's lunch. This might be a little trickier. We're approaching prime nap hours. We've probably been out and about most of the morning, wandering Betlemi's maze-like alleys or bargaining for Soviet-era movie posters at a local flea market. Our kids have been asked to admire things like churches and monuments, and to avoid things like street cats and lollipops they've found under a bench. But usually there are a few French fries floating around, and perhaps some pasta, so we get it done.

Dinner though – dinner is a dark, chaotic time. It's our Achilles heel, the Waterloo of meals. Battles are won and lost during dinner. Empires rise and fall. If we've inflicted ourselves on a restaurant, at least half of the people at our table and two members of the waiting staff cry during dinner. One of the four of us invariably gives up and just lies down on the floor. The bill has never taken so long to arrive. Dinner is a frantic, tear-filled descent into smeared peanut butter and actual spilled milk. No-one eats anything.

The problem with dinner is that it occurs at the very end of the day. It's the last hurdle before bedtime. The day has been long, and our toddler does not have the patience to wait for food or eat with silverware. We've admired four-hundred-year-old frescos inside Tbilisi's oldest church and hiked the ridge overlooking Narikala Fortress. Our children are baffled by our interest in 'very old buildings'. They are hot and tired, and adorable old Georgian ladies keep handing them flowers and pinching their cheeks. Staying in a hotel or guest house with a kitchenette makes eating dinner a little less of a spectacle, but that's not always possible.

Most evenings on the road we resort to what has become known as a 'floor picnic'. Doesn't that sound delicious? It's room service, first of all. Eating a $12 bowl of penne inside a hotel room absolutely violates all of our travel sensibilities. We are as disappointed in ourselves as you are, dear readers. But wait, it gets worse. Since there are four of us crammed inside one hotel room, all available surfaces have long been overtaken by piles of coats and hats and plastic trucks and extra blankets. So we eat on the floor, because toddlers and babies and sometimes adults are too messy to eat on a bed.

I know you probably think that there's nothing worse than a hotel room-service floor picnic, but you're wrong; there is exactly one thing worse than that. It's the inevitable result of desperately feeding your children the best parts of a $15 club sandwich and then immediately tucking them into bed. Suddenly it's seven o'clock, the lights are out, and if you make one single sound, the gremlins, who sleep through earthquakes and thunderstorms at home, will pop out of bed and immediately start asking for things like ice cream and orange juice and one more story.

So you do the unthinkable. You carry the remnants of your mangled sandwich into the bathroom and eat sitting on the edge of the bathtub, crying softly into an $8 beer, spreading hotel gift-store caviar on cold French fries, and promising yourself that this will never, ever happen again. Except it will – probably in about 24 hours.

We ate exactly one successful dinner in a restaurant during our six days in Georgia, dining at Bread House, a glorious, old brick building known for perfecting traditional Georgian cuisine and pairing it with an impressive collection of local wine. Located in the heart of the historic Abanotubani district, the restaurant's flagstone terrace and second-storey balcony overlook the meandering Mtkvari River. Just inside the entrance, an enormous clay oven – so round and deep as to appear like a well – churns out row after row of freshly baked bread. Here, a stone's throw from the city's renowned sulphur baths (enjoyed famously by two literary Alexanders, Dumas and Pushkin), we feasted on beef stew, grilled vegetables, cheese *khachapuri* and baskets on baskets of homemade bread. It was decadent, the weather perfect for *al fresco* dining.

There were two things that made that dinner possible, besides gorgeous weather. We started making or way to the restaurant at 4.45 p.m., rather than 6.00 p.m. when certain members of our family have long since transformed into ravenous goblins. And last, but never least, we were joined by a good friend who firmly tipped the balance in favour of the adults. Outnumbering the children is key for a meal in which everyone eats, at least a little, sitting and/or standing at the table while trying to prevent juice cups from falling on the floor and kids from scampering under the table.

If you ever find yourself in Tbilisi, eat at Bread House. And if you have kids with you, invite our friend Dave.

The daughter of an international businessman, **Jen Dowd** learned to globe-trot before she could walk. She's lived all over the world, but her favourite memories are of family vacations in Scotland, Egypt, and Syria. Now with two small children of her own, Jen is  carrying on the tradition. She is currently based in Cyprus, where she spends her time exploring the region, writing, and cultivating her own family's sense of adventure.

Next Stop, Camping

Lydia Unsworth

More than anywhere else at the moment, I want to go to the 'stans, to that whole ex-Soviet Central Asian expanse encompassing five modern countries, for which I've had a taste since first reading Kafka's *The Metamorphosis* and choosing Prague as my very first adult-life weekend city break (a three-day interlude that enabled me to peek behind the Iron Curtain at a history swamped by a completely different regime).

It's the nothingness I want. Great swathes of it. I want to be stifled by the scale of Kazakhstan, feel the breeze of unoccupied absence blowing about me, witness plants clawing their way patiently up the sides of untended concrete structures, see unmuffled traditions proudly back in centre frame.

With a toddler though, I wouldn't experience any of that. I'd be slap bang in the opposite of nothingness staring firmly at the back of my child's head as she bolts toward the nearest open gate.

There's a time for everything, and although I can't beat the wander bug out of the twenty-something's bedsheets, I can explore those neglected corners closer to home while my baby grows a little more accustomed to existing. At least until she can give a sound and honest opinion in response my incessant, wide-eyed 'How about Uzbekistan this summer?' suggestions.

When our baby was four months old, we rented a car and took her on a road trip through Belgium. She stayed in her first hostel, in a (thankfully otherwise unoccupied) four-bed dorm. I remember drinking a beer with my partner by the light of a headtorch on the lower bunk furthest from the crib on the floor to celebrate the end of another exhausting day. That trip was proof we could still adventure, proof that she was the adventure. Because having a baby and raising a person is an extreme sport.

What I didn't expect was how everything would be new. The way people smiled as I climbed the Atomium with a baby attached to me. The way I ascended the spiral staircase of a crumbling tower and the whole thing felt like I hadn't done it a hundred times before – and standing there at the top with my hand resting on the flank of a flint-sculpted phoenix, as I stared out at the ruffled Flemish countryside, I realised I could start again, turn the whole world over and begin anew.

We couchsurfed on that trip, staying at people's houses for free in return for company, kindness, humanitarian hope – people who also had children – and by way of this simple set up all us grown-ups who were temporarily, nocturnally housebound, we got to feel as if we were going out.

We went to a different town almost every day, finding different hosts, making friends and verbally exploring along the way. We entered homes, shared lives, swapped stories of children and travel and more. I met Belgian and French and Ukrainian and German children on that trip, saw the rhythm of their days; an experience that expanded my understanding of ways to mother far more effectively and honestly than a monthly prenatal meetup and some well-meaning but often slightly smug books.

A Polish friend I made through the website couchsurfing.com took her one-year-old along the Spanish pilgrimage route of the Camino de Santiago, taking 'walking the baby' to a whole new level.

Another friend went Interrailing with her little girl and sent me a link to the 'most accessible Alp for a two-year-old'. Positioning yourself near like-minded others is always reassuring, with your eyes peeled for flickers of charged and impassioned life.

The fullness I felt standing at the top of Mount Vesuvius last summer, with my one-year-old weighing down on my shoulders, on my chest. It was equal to a two-day trek through the Himalayas, equal to a night under the stars in the Thar Desert in Rajasthan. Sure, we took the tourist bus to the top and only walked the last twenty minutes to the peak, but first we had to work out how to get the train. Would it be full? Where were the lifts? How wide were the pavements along the way to the station? Did we have enough clothes, enough food, enough nappies? Water? Milk? Suncream? A book (just in case)? Did we have the cuddly owl? The hat? Enough change for the tickets? Where was the ticket desk, or ticket machine? At what stop should we get off? Which way to the Vesuvius bus stop? How hot would it be? Could we leave our buggy somewhere safe? – and that walk of twenty minutes contained an extra ten kilos from which we could not take a break.

Travelling with a little one: it's wild, it's intense and it's continuous. Like diving in a rubber ring and setting off down the rapids, while trying to process a VAT return along the way. It's also ridiculous, it frees me from my self, from my former constraints. Life on the move is like an ongoing escape room: a series of back-to-back problems to be solved and only a minute to sort each of them out. And then the rewards. An even bigger series of unexpected moments, encounters and solutions that flex every muscle of my mind and heart. The kindness I see in every country I visit with my daughter, although also to be found when hitch-hiking, when lost, when lonely or nervous in the land of solo backpacking, is made all that more heightened by my relative mothering inexperience and by the lack of anonymity that comes with a bold and screaming child.

I freely walked through a shopping mall on my most recent trip with my now-toddler, covered in urine from my breast to my belly, on the way to a soft-play centre to break up the sightseeing of the afternoon. I washed my wee-drenched top with liquid hand soap in the nearest toilets, dried myself off with toilet roll, and hung the top in the narrow slot of the intensive hand dryer until it seemed dry enough to put back on. I like the surprises. I like the need to figure out the best next thing to do.

I like that appearances fade away in the eye of the problem, insecurity diminishes, and my body and trust in myself become strong. People become kinder, braver, sillier, more informal, all in the presence of a child, all in the presence of a struggling parent. Budget flights are now a source of community rather than a test of endurance. I didn't expect to find this whole new world of goodness. I have my baby to thank.

Next stop, camping. Then, after that, maybe the 'stans.

Lydia Unsworth is the Manchester and Amsterdam-based author of two collections of poetry: *Certain Manoeuvres* (Knives Forks & Spoons, 2018) and *Nostalgia for Bodies* (Erbacce, 2018), for which she won the 2018 Erbacce Poetry Prize. Her work can be found in *Ambit, Pank, Litro, Tears in the Fence, Banshee, Ink Sweat and Tears* and *Sentence: Journal of Prose Poetics*. Lydia was also longlisted for the Women Poets' Prize 2018. She tweets at @lydiowanie.

The Faraway Family Tree

Kirstie Pelling

Our story starts here in a faraway tree,
where a cloud carousel of enchanting new lands
bowls a moon from a sky. Climb up high, take my hand,
adventure land's near. A 'must see.'
Peg a tent to its core. Make a fire with snow
lit with kindling of spring. Travel free from the source
to the sea, from toddler to teen, on a course
with an ending we know.
Dodge shadows and shallows in rivers. Drip dry
under skies dipped in gold. Swallows fly. Don't catch cold,
catch a spark from a star as it burns out and folds.
Murmurations of moments slip by.
Zip wire on rainbows, a prism of the years
makes light of your tears. You experiment and trust.
Summer follows the swallows. Yesterday is dusk
and the dark holds no fears.
Hush! Hear the rush
of a land moving on? Be gone.
Forge a path. Grow your own family.
Listen out for the whisper of a faraway tree.
When new lands swing by, take the kids. Think of me.

Kirstie Pelling is a writer and journalist living in Cumbria. She has spent two decades adventuring with her husband and three children in the outdoors. Together they have tackled everything from long-distance cycle tours of multiple countries to doorstep micro-adventures in the Lakes and fells. Their

award winning blog **w** familyadventureproject.org documents their travels and aims to inspire other families to get out and enjoy the world together.

Now read on...

We hope you have enjoyed the stories in *Kidding Around*. This is the fifth of our anthologies of wild and wonderful travellers' tales. On the following pages you'll find extracts from the previous four.

Save £10.99! Get one book free when you buy all four previous Bradt travel writing anthologies at w bradtguides.com. See page 226 for full details.

The Irresponsible Traveller
9781841625621 £10.99

Seasoned travellers, including Michael Palin, Ben Fogle and Jonathan Scott, recount exciting, often dangerous predicaments they've found themselves in, from being accosted by Brazilian kidnappers to a midnight raid to free turtles on the Amazon.

"This is what it's like to be chased. I skid around another bend, my lights panning over the chicane and out to distant rainforest on the far side of the valley. The wheels squeal. The rain is falling in sheets now. And they're still behind me, right on my tail, their black pick-up weaving and bobbing in the rear-view mirror, desperate to overtake and block the road again.

I floor the accelerator and the tiny Fiat engine revs so hard it sounds like its pistons will burst, the road lines flashes of light in the glistening black. The car claws back a precious few metres from my pursuers. Then they speed up, swerve to the left and are level with me. Their window's down. The driver's shouting across the narrow gap, his face explosive with rage. *'Para o carro filho da puta!'* Stop the car! But I've accelerated just enough. I'm into the next bend. They brake hard and are behind me once again.

It's got to be soon. Paraty's got to be soon!

But there's still no sign of the town. No lights through the rain. No life. No headlights approaching the other way. No... wait. What's that? There's a shimmer through the trees, just round the next bend. I floor the accelerator again and leap into the corner, the car lurching towards the precipice at the edge of the road before swinging violently back into another straight. I see a single light – four hundred metres away. A house? Three hundred... There's a sign, 'Mecânico', dripping with rain. Two hundred... Yes! A house. That means people. One hundred... I swing in and pull to a halt, horn blaring. Someone's bound to emerge. The pick-up will whizz past.

It doesn't. And the house stays quiet. I'm caught. The pick-up pulls in behind me, headlamps blazing. They get out. Big black pistols in their hands, right index fingers on the triggers. Left index fingers across their lips."

From Road Trip by Alex Robinson

"I'm not asleep though, and neither is Louise. Hardly surprising, what with the nodding cranium of our companion Dennis thudding into her left shoulder at every jolt of the rails. Upright, anxious, her eyes glint in the carriage's one weak overhead light. 'Now,' she hisses. 'Do it now.'

I get to my feet and, for the umpteenth time, scan up and down the carriage. Nobody appears to be watching. There's no sign of movement. The border guards are far behind us – even now staggering out of some shebeen, no doubt, or tucked up in bed, dreaming of sniffer dogs and smugglers.

The aisle is an obstacle course. I manoeuvre over outstretched legs and hefty baggage, steadying myself against the sway to avoid accidentally grabbing a sleeping face. A judder prompts one snorer to grunt and shift, stopping me dead. False alarm: the carriage remains insensible to my progress. Reaching the end, I pass into the interim corridor, stepping over a film-reel blur of tracks beneath the gap at my feet, and find myself standing between the closed doors of two toilets. Mine is the one to the left. I grasp the handle.

But wait. Suppose they're watching me. Suppose they know exactly what I've done and are lying in ambush. One more step and the night will explode into lights, yells, whistles and uniforms. They'll have me red-handed."

From Something to Declare by Mike Unwin

To Oldly Go
9781784770273 £10.99

Remarkable travel tales from 'silver travellers', including Dervla Murphy travelling in Cuba at the age of 74, Matthew Parris swimming the Thames at 60 and Colin Thubron climbing the last stronghold of the Assassins in his 60s.

"I saw her immediately as I disembarked from the cruise ship: an attractive lady of around thirty watching the mostly over-sixties arrive on Saint Petersburg's quay, most of them looking for coaches to take them to the prescribed sights of the city. She stood quietly, with a self-confidence based on her attractiveness as well as being in her home territory and knowing the ropes. I guessed she was waiting for a single male to approach her."

"I walked up to the lady, remembering the Russian custom of not smiling.

'How much do you charge and for how long?'

With the barest suggestion of friendliness in her face, she quoted fifty US dollars for up to two hours. I later discovered that she was an English teacher in a local comprehensive school at basic secondary level. So I instructed Anya on what I wanted for the fifty bucks and in less than two hours.

I want to see three things in the city, travelling by taxi, I told her, and would like to ask questions as we go. I would like to travel through the poorest part of Saint Petersburg and see the homes there. I would like to travel through the richest residential part of the city. Lastly, with your permission, I would like to see where you live, the food you eat, the ingredients you choose and cooking utensils you use and the books you read.

Cocking her head to one side, she asked, 'Is that very all?'

'Yes, very completely definitely all.'"

From *Changing the World's Oldest Profession*
by Arnold Shirek Chamove

"A few days ago I was standing in a lay-by, feeling a little foolish – as one does – with my thumb out, watching drivers lean forward in their seats to stare intently before deciding no, and speeding on.

No-one does it these days, they tell me, but I'm proud to say that I've hitchhiked every decade of my life except the first. And I'm in my seventies. I hitch when there is no alternative, as was the case last week, but I also hitch because it's the best way I know to meet thoroughly decent people and reaffirm my trust in the human race. I also think it's interesting to experience the shifting ground between control and helplessness.

For my generation, hitchhiking was part of life. We all did it. As youngsters, few of us had cars and public transport was expensive. If we wanted to travel abroad we hitchhiked and competed over who could spend the least amount of money on their holiday. When a friend and I travelled to the Middle East in 1963, we were honour-bound never to pay for transport. Nor did we need to.

Then I moved to America and assumed that my hitchhiking days were over. All Americans have cars, don't they? So I was in for a shock when I starting dating a man who not only had no car, but assumed that I would hitch everywhere with him. I didn't like to say no, so there I was, in my thirties, exploring America through the kindness of strangers. And such extravagant kindness! One driver just pointed out his house, got out of the car and said, 'You kids go see this place. Just bring the car back later this evening.' Yes, we were kids to him.

As I continued to seek the occasional lift in my forties and fifties, the drivers must have got a nasty shock when they stopped and realised that this hitchhiker was getting on in years. But it was only when I started travelling with Janice, who is two years older than me and has white hair, that I discovered the advantages of flaunting, rather than concealing, your age."

From *Thumbs Up* by Hilary Bradt

Roam Alone
9781784770495 £10.99
Stories from travellers who overcame their reservations to strike out alone. Foreword by Jan Leeming.

"The following year I had a close call with cancer and when I didn't die within the predicted year, I resolved to go back to India. No-one would or could come with me so, pig-headedly, I said I'd go on my own. It was an easy thing to say, but could I really go alone? Really *on my own*? After I'd said goodbye to my husband at Heathrow, I went into the ladies and sobbed. What was I doing?

I had never travelled on my own. When we went abroad on holiday I had never even used the foreign currency – I was petrified. So I had cheated a little and booked the first ten days with a small group adventure travel company to help me get over my initial nerves. We spent those first ten days travelling to Kochi, Mysore and Ootacamund; then I said goodbye and headed alone for the railway station in Bangalore to catch the overnight train to Hampi.

This fascinating historical site, set in a strange and beautiful, boulder-strewn landscape, was in fact the perfect place for me to explore for the first time completely on my own. Each day my confidence grew and with it my sense of awareness and safety. What was I doing? Was it respectful? A deserted restaurant was probably not as safe as a full one. I learned to trust my gut feeling when it came to judging people. I found that all these long-buried skills, which we all possess, were slowly getting stronger. And before I left there, I'd even found myself part of a Bollywood movie."

From Really? On My Own? by Sandra Reekie

"I arrived trying to suppress my unconscious negativity towards Russians, but a minute in I had already failed. A man came up to me wearing a sign saying he was a taxi driver. I immediately told him no. He had the same cold face of every terrorist and kidnapper I was ever warned about from movies and television shows. I tried to find the bus I had read about, but I was very lost and so when he offered again I said yes. The more confused I looked, I thought, the more vulnerable I was and it was time for a decision. As my heart raced, I followed him out and I heard every relative and friend of mine telling me to turn back.

I was so stupid and this was why I shouldn't have come. I checked to see if it was a marked cab. It was, and the other drivers knew him and even let out a greeting as he passed. There wasn't a single reason not to trust him, but I was still on edge. I got in and waited to be driven to some far-off place and never be heard from again.

Then he was on the phone – telling his friends, I was sure, that he had tricked a stupid foreigner. He started talking to me, yelling about something and pointing to the door. I rolled down the window. That was wrong. He pointed again and I looked down. A tourist map and brochures. I looked through them. You would think at this point I'd be over my irrational fear, but I was still convinced that this was all a ploy to trick me and that he was still planning on robbing me or worse. Then he started talking again, and he asked if I spoke English. I said yes and he began yelling into his phone's translator. He showed me the word: 'present'. I assumed he wanted the money now – the only logical explanation – and handed him 2,000 rubles. He waved me away and pointed. Now I got it. The brochures were for me to keep.

His next translation was 'low-water bridge', and boy, was there a low-water bridge. The bridge was so close to the water we were almost gliding on top of it and I was able to look across the bay at the sunset. He rolled the window down so I could take a good photo. It was my first glimpse of the beauty I would continue to encounter in the most unexpected places here. Then he started pointing to the right and saying some words in Russian that I couldn't understand. I thought that must be where he was going to pull over and lead me to my death, now that he had my trust. But no, he rolled the window down again so I could take a picture of what he had been pointing to – a monastery.

We passed under a large crest and he motioned with his hands and said 'Vladivostok'. We were now in the city and the crest of a tiger, he explained, was its symbol. At this time, the taxi driver introduced himself as Alexander and asked me my name. As we passed various places he would say, 'Nicole, Nicole,' and point to the best photo spots. He turned around in his seat and opened the map I had, pointing out the sights. We soon neared a spot marked with a camera and he yelled at me, 'Photo! Photo!' I saw the most incredible view of the Golden Horn Bridge, Vladivostok's new marvel spanning the bay. I suddenly felt embarrassed and a little ashamed. He was the kindest cab driver I'd ever known. And yet I had taken him to be a crook. I had a lot to learn."

From *Taxi Ride in Vladivostok* by Nicole Teufel

Beastly Journeys
9781784770815 £10.99

A compendium of extraordinary animal travel experiences, from hilarious holidays with pets to journeys on which wild animals somehow came along for the ride, including: David Attenborough tries to get an armadillo through Paraguayan customs; adventurer Ash Dykes takes a white cockerel to Maromokotro to ward off evil spirits; Brian Jackman rides, walks and swims with Abu the elephant, and John Rendall travels to Africa with Christian, the lion he bought at Harrods.

"When did Barry first enter my life? Let me think. Well, he may have been with our group when Fredy led us into the swamp on the hunt for anacondas. Or when we took that night walk through the grasping foliage and Fredy had to rescue us all from the herd of wild pigs. Yes, perhaps he was there then. But perhaps not. The truth is I've no idea now. That's the rainforest for you; it can hypnotise a callow tourist with flurrying parakeets and howler monkeys booming from misty treetops so that time becomes nothing but a series of vivid moments, like bulb flashes at the backs of your eyes.

Let's just say we came together at some point during that four-day expedition, and for a while we were inseparable. We remained together on the river journey back out of the jungle and on the flight home to the UK. I took him on walks around my local haunts, on evenings out in town, and to the Cotswolds when I visited my mother over the bank holiday weekend. He even shared my bed.

And then, on a Saturday morning, as I sat dreaming in a chair, Barry poked his head out of my leg."

From *Barry's Flying Visit* by Adrian Phillips

"I threw down my bike and ran screaming towards the dogs with a force I'd never known. Everything happened within seconds as a blur, kicking and pulling the dogs off, still screaming, until they ran away. She was lying on her side. I knelt down, tears filled my eyes. I spoke softly to her that everything was going to be OK. She moved her head just enough to lick my hand. Her big chocolate-brown eyes looked into mine and melted my heart. In that moment, I named her 'Lucy'. She needed my help, just like I had needed help all those years ago. 'You're a good girl,' I said.

I decided then I'd take her to a dog sanctuary where she'd be cared for. The only problem was that it was hundreds of kilometres away. And so I'd stood looking at the already fully loaded bicycle thinking, *Wow, I have to somehow fit a twenty-kilogram dog on there too, and then cycle it.* I walked the bicycle and Lucy to the outskirts of the next town, and stopped at what looked like a hardware store. I motioned to the shop assistant to come over and if charades were a featured discipline in the Olympics, my performance would have been gold medal worthy. The shop assistant returned carrying a thin wooden vegetable crate, metal wire and pliers.

I removed the luggage hanging over my front wheel and strapped it to the sides of the rear bags, then knelt down and began attaching the crate to the front of the bike with wire. Within seconds, my hands were black and my face too from wiping sweat from my brow. Local residents had begun watching the show on their pavement. Word was spreading the box was for the dog. My hands began to bleed from the wire and the oil mixed in with the blood. Finishing, I stood up and wiped my hands on my floral skirt, which was exactly why I'd chosen such a pattern. I touched the crate and it rocked slightly from side to side. Well, this was the best I could do in this moment with what I had. I cushioned the inside of the crate with cycling tops, making sure the red tartan Scottish one was to the top. I knew my dog carrier was a bit wobbly, but I was amazed I had done it all by myself. I stood back looking at the bike, box and Lucy. This was never going to work, but I had no choice."

From *Me, My Bike and a Street Dog Called Lucy* by **Ishbel Holmes**

Order online and get a free book

Special offer on the Bradt Travel Writing Anthologies.
When you buy three of our travel writing anthologies, we'll give you the fourth one for free. Simply add one copy each of *The Irresponsible Traveller*, *To Oldly Go*, *Roam Alone* and *Beastly Journeys* to your shopping cart and you will automatically be given one book for free.

bradtguides.com/shop